ORACLE AND MYSQL

A Practical Approach

ORACLE AND MYSQL

A Practical Approach

By

B. Mohamed Ibrahim

MCA., M.Phil., MBA.,

Software Technical Consultant

FIREWALL MEDIA

(An Imprint of Laxmi Publications Pvt. Ltd.)

BANGALORE • CHENNAI • COCHIN • GUWAHATI • HYDERABAD
JALANDHAR • KOLKATA • LUCKNOW • MUMBAI • RANCHI
NEW DELHI • BOSTON, USA

Published by :

FIREWALL MEDIA

(*An Imprint of Laxmi Publications Pvt. Ltd.*)
113, Golden House, Daryaganj,
New Delhi-110002

Phone : 011-43 53 25 00
Fax : 011-43 53 25 28

www.laxmipublications.com
info@laxmipublications.com

First Edition : 2013

OFFICES

✆ **Bangalore**	080-26 75 69 30	✆ **Chennai**	044-24 34 47 26
✆ **Cochin**	0484-237 70 04, 405 13 03	✆ **Guwahati**	0361-251 36 69, 251 38 81
✆ **Hyderabad**	040-24 65 23 33	✆ **Jalandhar**	0181-222 12 72
✆ **Kolkata**	033-22 27 43 84	✆ **Lucknow**	0522-220 99 16
✆ **Mumbai**	022-24 91 54 15, 24 92 78 69	✆ **Ranchi**	0651-221 47 64

FOR-3082-125-ORACLE & MYSQL-IBR

Typeset at : Sukuvisa Enterprises, New Delhi.

CONTENTS

PREFACE

The Database Management System (DBMS) is a software product that organises the storage and retrieval of data with database. Major developments are going on in the DBMS field to achieve the required security, integrity of data and easy to work with it. Those developments include: RDBMS (Relational Database Management System), OODMS (Object Oriented Database Management System), and ORDBMS (Object RDBMS).

Oracle is the most widely used RDBMS, and MySQL is the most popular open-source RDBMS. Both of these databases provide support for database connectivity to high-level languages. This book focuses on these two database systems, with basics to intermediate level.

Chapter 1 (Introduction to Database Systems): This chapter introduces the basic concepts of databases. The features of Relational DBMS, various types of keys used in database design are explored. The Normalization process is explained in detail with the Normal Forms. Suitable example queries with their corresponding output are given for easy understanding of concepts.

Chapter 2 (Working with Oracle Database): This chapter is devoted for Oracle database. This chapter starts with Oracle Installation. The SQL commands are grouped as Data Definition Language (DDL), Data Manipulation Language (DML) and Transaction Control Language (TCL) commands and explained with example queries. The database objects such as views, synonyms, and sequences are explained with their general formats. The PL/SQL for Oracle is explained in detail with sample code. The stored procedures are neatly explained, which can be called by an application through database connectivity to minimise database interactions in performing bulk database operations. Some basic database administrative operations such as creating databases, creating users, back-up and restore databases, grant and revoke privileges on database are given.

Chapter 3 (Working with MySQL Database): This chapter explains the important concepts to work with MySQL database. This chapter started with the MySQL installation procedure for Microsoft Windows platform. Important data-definition, data-manipulation, transaction-control, and MySQL programs are explained with illustrations. A set of frequently used built-in functions are given by their operations wise. The latest features of MySQL, stored procedures / functions, triggers, are explained with example code.

This book is intensely written for the beginners and intermediates in database knowledge, and those are using databases in high-level languages for developing applications. It is written in a practical approach that the readers will find suitable example code with output wherever they expect them.

I thank the Almighty Allah, who gave me the soul, strength, knowledge and everything. All praise is due to him. Salutations on the Prophet (may Allah's blessings and peace be upon him) and his descendents. I thank all the well wishers of mine, who prayed the Almighty for me.

—Author

Chapter 1

Introduction to Database Systems

1.0 INTRODUCTION

A datum represents a raw fact and figure, a meaningful datum gives information. A group of related data forms a record. A file is composed of several related records. A database is an integrated collection of related files. The Database Management System (DBMS) is a software product that organises the storage and retrieval of data with database. Major developments are going on in the DBMS field to achieve the required security, integrity of data and easy to work with it. Those developments include: RDBMS (Relational Database Management System), OODMS (Object Oriented Database Management System), and ORDBMS (Object RDBMS). This chapter briefs the basic database concepts.

1.1 RDBMS

The Database Management System (DBMS) is a concept to store, access, and manipulate the data in an effective way. Generally the data are stored in the format of tables (records), comprised of rows (tuple) and columns (attributes); these tables form a database. To make relational (compare and combine) operations on database tables, the Relational Database Management System (RDBMS) is designed. Popular RDBMS software include *Oracle*, *MySQL*, *MS SQL Server*, *Sybase*, and *Informix*. Every RDBMS software should satisfy the following rules, defined by Boyce and Codd (also called as Boyce-Codd rules). However, conflicts are still there that some of the RDBMS software do not satisfy all these twelve rules.

Boyce-codd rules:

1. The information rule
2. The rule of guaranteed access

3. The systematic treatment of all *null* values
4. The database description rule
5. The comprehensive data sub language rule
6. The view updating rule
7. The insert and update rule
8. The physical data independence rule
9. The logical data independence rule
10. The integrity independence rule
11. The distribution rule
12. No sub version rule.

1.2 DATABASE KEYS

The database keys are used to keep the database records straight, and forms structure of database tables. There are many keys defined in database, some important and frequently referred keys are briefed as below.

Key: A key is a single or combination of attributes in a database table.

Primary Key: An attribute or a combination of attributes that uniquely identifies a record in a database table.

Unique Key: It a constraint that is applied on an attribute or a combination of attributes for uniquely identifying the values in that column(s), but the column(s) can accept NULL values.

Difference between Primary Key and Unique Key: Primary key will not accept NULL values, however Unique key will accept.

Composite Key/Concatenate Key: A primary key that made up of more than one attributes.

Foreign Key: A primary key can be references to another table as a Foreign Key. An attribute or a combination of attributes in a table which matches a primary key in another table.

Composite Primary Key: A Primary key consists of a combination of attributes (more than one column).

Super Key: A Super Key is a combination of attributes that can be uniquely used to identify a database record. A table may have many Super Keys.

Candidate Key: A candidate key is an attribute/a combination of attributes that can be uniquely used to identify a database without any extraneous information. A Candidate Keys are a sub-set of Super Keys that do not have any extraneous information in them. Each table may have one or more candidate keys. Primary key for the table is selected from these candidate keys. Any of the candidate key that is not part of the primary key is called Alternate Key.

Surrogate Key: It is just a unique value in each record that uniquely identifies the record and act as a primary key. The only requirement for a surrogate primary key is that it is unique for each row in the table. These Surrogate keys are not derived from application data; it is generally generated by RDBMS itself such as Sequences (Oracle), Auto Increment (MySQL), UUIDs (Universal Unique Identifiers), and GUIDs (Globally Unique Identifiers).

1.3 NORMALIZATION

"Normalization is the optimisation process of efficiently organizing data in a database so that redundancy of data will be eliminated, data dependencies will be ensured and data confirms to the defined integrity constraints."

Data dependency includes grouping only strongly related data in a table (for example, in employee table, one can store employee_number, employee_name, salary, etc., but not project_duration. The integrity constraints ensure the adherence of defined rules on data, for example, the mark column in marklist table should accept value within the range 0-100.

The Readers who are new to database may find difficulties in understanding the SQL statements used in the examples with the following sections. Please refer forth-coming chapters for detailed explanation of SQL statements.

1.3.1 Normal Forms

They are the rules and guidelines to make ensure a database is normalized.

1.3.1.1 First Normal Form (1NF)

"A database table is in the first normal form if it contains only atomic values."

Focus: Eliminate repeating groups/group value in fields.

Atomic values refer no repeating groups (set of columns of same kind of data, for example, email1, email2 ... and address1, address2 ...), no group of fields (group of filed: the value with divisible parts, for example, address column contains a group value which can be divisible to door_number, street_name, city_name, country_name, postal_code ...).

Example:

Note: I am using SQL Client command-line interface for executing SQL statements.

```
SQL> create table employee (
     empnumber number(5) primary key,
     empname   varchar2(30),
     salary    number(9,2),
     emails    varchar2(100)
     );
Table created.
SQL> insert into employee (empnumber, empname, salary, emails) values
     (1001, 'Mohamed Ibrahim', 92000.0,
     'bmohamedibrahim@yahoo.co.in, bmdibrahim@rediffmail.com');
1 row created.
SQL> select * from employee;
EMPNUMBER EMPNAME          SALARY EMAILS
---- --------------- ----- -------------------------------------------------------
1001 Mohamed Ibrahim 92000 bmohamedibrahim@yahoo.co.in, bmdibrahim@rediffmail.com
```

The above employee table contains non-atomic value for the columns emails and empname. The emails filed contains many email addresses (in our example, two emails) separated by comma.

The empname filed contains both first name and last name. We can change the design of the above table as below:

```
SQL> drop table employee;
Table dropped.

SQL> create table employee
     ( empnumber      number(4) primary key,
     empfirstname     varchar2(16),
     emplastname      varchar2(16),
     salary           number(9,2),
     email1           varchar2(50),
     email2           varchar2(50)
     );
Table created.

SQL> insert into employee (empnumber, empfirstname, emplastname,
     salary, email1, email2) values
     (1001, 'Mohamed', 'Ibrahim', 92000.0,
     'bmohamedibrahim@yahoo.co.in', 'bmdibrahim@rediffmail.com');
1 row created.
```

In the above table, even though no group of values present in columns, repeating groups occurred. The columns email1 and email2 are repeating groups. We can use a separate table to store email addresses and map them with our employee table using foreign key reference as below.

```
SQL> create table employee
     ( empnumber        number(4) primary key,
     empfirstname       varchar2(16),
     emplastname        varchar2(16),
     salary             number(9,2)
     );
Table created.

SQL> create table email_address
     ( id             number(5) primary key,
     email            varchar2(50),
     empnumber        number(5),
     foreign key      (empnumber) references employee(empnumber)
                                          on delete cascade
     );
Table created.

SQL> insert into employee (empnumber, empfirstname, emplastname,
     salary) values(1001, 'Mohamed', 'Ibrahim', 92000.0);
1 row created.
```

```
SQL> insert into email_address (id, email, empnumber) values
     (1, 'bmohamedibrahim@yahoo.co.in', 1001);
1 row created.

SQL> insert into email_address (id, email, empnumber) values
     (2, 'bmdibrahim@rediffmail.com', 1001);
1 row created.

SQL> select * from employee;
     EMPNUMBER    EMPFIRSTNAME   EMPLASTNAME     SALARY
     ----------   ------------   ------------    ----------
     1001         Mohamed        Ibrahim         92000

SQL> select * from email_address;
       ID EMAIL                              EMPNUMBER
------ ---------------------------           ----------
        1 bmohamedibrahim@yahoo.co.in        1001
        2 bmdibrahim@rediffmail.com          1001
```

1.3.1.2 Second Normal Form (2NF)

"A database table is in the second normal form if it fulfils all the requirements of the first normal form and all non-primary-key fields in the table must be fully dependent on the entire primary key of the table."

Focus: Eliminate redundant data on non-primary and non-foreign key fields.

The entire primary key refers the whole set of fields of composite primary key. The 2NF enforces no partial dependencies. The 2NF further forces to remove duplicate values in the columns of a table.

The composite primary key is a primary key in a table made up of more than one column. In the following example, we are defining the combination of firstname and lastname in employee table as composite primary key, so that duplicate values on either firstname or lastname are allowed, but a duplicate value on the combination of these two fields are not allowed.

```
SQL> drop table email_address;
Table dropped.

SQL> drop table employee;
Table dropped.

SQL> create table employee
     (firstname  varchar2(16),
     lastname    varchar2(16),
     salary      number(9,2),
```

```
     constraint  employee_pk primary key (firstname, lastname)
     );
Table created.

SQL> insert into employee (firstname, lastname, salary) values
     ('mohamed', 'ibrahim', 98000.0);
1 row created.

SQL> insert into employee (firstname, lastname, salary) values
     ('mohamed', 'yasin', 87000.0);
1 row created.

SQL> insert into employee (firstname, lastname, salary) values
     ('syed', 'ibrahim', 82500.0);
1 row created.

SQL> select * from employee;
     FIRSTNAME      LASTNAME       SALARY
     ----------     ---------      ----------
     mohamed        ibrahim        98000
     mohamed        yasin          87000
     syed           ibrahim        82500

SQL> insert into employee (firstname, lastname, salary) values
     ('syed', 'ibrahim', 50000.0);
insert into employee (firstname, lastname, salary) values
*
ERROR at line 1:
ORA-00001: unique constraint (IBRAHIM.EMPLOYEE_PK) violated
```

Example

Now, let us take one example to illustrate second normal form.

```
SQL> create table teacher_info
     ( teacher_id          number(4),
     teacher_first_name    varchar2(16),
     teacher_last_name     varchar2(16),
     class_id              varchar2(4),
     class_name            varchar2(40),
     constraint teacher_info_pk primary key (teacher_id, class_id)
     );
Table created.

SQL> insert into teacher_info (teacher_id, teacher_first_name,
     teacher_last_name, class_id, class_name)
```

```
    values (1001, 'Mohamed', 'Ibrahim', 'CS', 'Computer Science');
1 row created.

SQL> insert into teacher_info (teacher_id, teacher_first_name,
    teacher_last_name, class_id, class_name)
    values (1002, 'Mohamed', 'Yaseen', 'CS', 'Computer Science');
1 row created.

SQL> insert into teacher_info (teacher_id, teacher_first_name,
    teacher_last_name, class_id, class_name)
    values (1003, 'Karan', 'Singh', 'MGT', 'Management');
1 row created.

SQL> insert into teacher_info (teacher_id, teacher_first_name,
    teacher_last_name, class_id, class_name)
    values (1003, 'Karan', 'Singh', 'COM', 'Commerce');
1 row created.

SQL> insert into teacher_info (teacher_id, teacher_first_name,
    teacher_last_name, class_id, class_name)
    values (1004, 'Kiran', 'Kumar', 'COM', 'Commerce');
1 row created.

SQL> insert into teacher_info (teacher_id, teacher_first_name,
    teacher_last_name, class_id, class_name)
    values (1005, 'Akhfa', 'Nafi', 'COM', 'Commerce');
1 row created.

SQL> insert into teacher_info (teacher_id, teacher_first_name,
    teacher_last_name, class_id, class_name)
    values (1006, 'Ravi', 'Chandren', 'MGT', 'Management');
1 row created.

SQL> insert into teacher_info (teacher_id, teacher_first_name,
    teacher_last_name, class_id, class_name)
    values (1007, 'Nitin', 'Otageri', 'ZOO', 'Zoology');
1 row created.

SQL> select * from teacher_info;
    TEACHER_ID TEACHER_FIRST_NA TEACHER_LAST_NAM CLAS CLASS_NAME
    ---------- ---------------- ---------------- ---- ----------------
    1001       Mohamed          Ibrahim          CS   Computer Science
    1002       Mohamed          Yaseen           CS   Computer Science
```

```
      1003      Karan      Singh      MGT   Management
      1003      Karan      Singh      COM   Commerce
      1004      Kiran      Kumar      COM   Commerce
      1005      Akhfa      Nafi       COM   Commerce
      1006      Ravi       Chandren   MGT   Management
      1007      Nitin      Otageri    ZOO   Zoology
8 rows selected.
```

In the above `employee` table, the combination of `teacher_id` and `class_id` forms primary key. The value in the non-key (no key set on the column) column `class_name` is repeated and it is dependent on `class_id` as the `class_name` is repeated for each repeated `class_id`, but it not dependent on `teacher_id`, *i.e.*, the column `class_name` is partially dependent on the primary key.

Some limitations of the above design of employee table:

- Changes should be made on individual records. Suppose if you want to change the `class_name` name "`Computer Science`" to "`Information Technology`", then we have to change in record by record. In our example, we have to change in two records.
- Add and Removal of individual group (without dependent on another group) is expensive. Suppose if you want to add a `class_name` named "`Botany`" having `class_id` "**`BOT`**" without any teachers (assume that the teachers will be added later), you can't add as the `teacher_id` field cannot be `null` while insertion. What happen when you delete an employee who is *only* belonging to a department? Then, no more that department in the table. In our example database, if we delete record of teacher_id 1007, then the department 'Zoology' is no more in the database.

The following is the database design for the above table using 2NF which eliminates repeating data on non-key fields using foreign-key references (Note that the foreign-key filed is the only filed which can contain repeated values to refer multiple records). Thus, it groups related fields in separate tables and every non-key field become dependent fully on primary key.

```
SQL> create table teacher
     ( id            number(4),
     first_name      varchar2(16),
     last_name       varchar2(16),
     constraint      teacher_pk primary key (id)
     );
Table created.

SQL> create table class
     ( id            varchar2(4),
     class_name      varchar2(40),
     constraint      class_pk primary key (id)
     );
Table created.
```

```
SQL> create table teacher_class_mapping
     ( teacher_id  number(4) references teacher(id),
     class_id      varchar2(4) references class(id),
     constraint    teacher_class_mapping_pk primary key
                               (teacher_id, class_id)
     );
Table created.

SQL> insert into teacher (id, first_name, last_name) values
     (1001, 'Mohamed', 'Ibrahim');
1 row created.

SQL> insert into teacher (id, first_name, last_name) values
     (1002, 'Mohamed', 'Yaseen');
1 row created.

SQL> insert into teacher (id, first_name, last_name) values
     (1003, 'Karan', 'Singh');
1 row created.

SQL> insert into teacher (id, first_name, last_name) values
     (1004, 'Kiran', 'Kumar');
1 row created.

SQL> insert into teacher (id, first_name, last_name) values
     (1005, 'Akhfa', 'Nafi');
1 row created.

SQL> insert into teacher (id, first_name, last_name) values
     (1006, 'Ravi', 'Chandren');
1 row created.

SQL> insert into teacher (id, first_name, last_name) values
     (1007, 'Nitin', 'Otageri');
1 row created.

SQL> insert into class (id, class_name)
     values ('IT', 'Information Technology');
1 row created.

SQL> insert into class (id, class_name)
     values ('CS', 'Computer Science');
1 row created.
```

```
SQL> insert into class (id, class_name)
     values ('MGT', 'Management');
1 row created.

SQL> insert into class (id, class_name)
     values ('COM', 'Commerce');
1 row created.

SQL> insert into class (id, class_name)
     values ('ZOO', 'Zoology');
1 row created.

SQL> insert into teacher_class_mapping (teacher_id, class_id) values
     (1001, 'IT');
1 row created.

SQL> insert into teacher_class_mapping (teacher_id, class_id) values
     (1002, 'CS');
1 row created.

SQL> insert into teacher_class_mapping (teacher_id, class_id) values
     (1003, 'MGT');
1 row created.

SQL> insert into teacher_class_mapping (teacher_id, class_id) values
     (1004, 'COM');
1 row created.

SQL> insert into teacher_class_mapping (teacher_id, class_id) values
     (1005, 'ZOO');
1 row created.

SQL> select * from teacher;
          ID   FIRST_NAME     LAST_NAME
     -------   ------------   ----------------
        1001   Mohamed        Ibrahim
        1002   Mohamed        Yaseen
        1003   Karan          Singh
        1004   Kiran          Kumar
        1005   Akhfa          Nafi
        1006   Ravi           Chandren
        1007   Nitin          Otageri
7 rows selected.
```

```
SQL> select * from class;
     ID     CLASS_NAME
     ----   ------------------------
     IT     Information Technology
     CS     Computer Science
     MGT    Management
     COM    Commerce
     ZOO    Zoology

SQL> select * from teacher_class_mapping;
     TEACHER_ID  CLAS
     ----------  ----
           1001  IT
           1002  CS
           1003  MGT
           1004  COM
           1005  ZOO
```

1.3.1.3 Third Normal Form (3NF)

"A database table is in the third normal form if it fulfils all the requirements of the second normal form and no transitive dependencies in the table, as no non-primary key filed is transitively dependent on primary key".

Focus: Eliminate dependencies on Non-Key fields by eliminating fields that are not depending on primary key.

Transitive relationship: For the relation R, if aRb and bRc, then aRc. That is, if a is related to b and b is related to c, then a is related to c.

Transitive dependency: A transitive dependency is a dependency in which the value in a non-key field is determined by the value in another non-key field and the value in that filed is determined by the value in the primary key field. In other words, a non-key field is dependent on another non-key field which is dependent on the primary key.

Example:

```
SQL> create table teacher_info
     ( teacher_id           number(4),
     teacher_first_name   varchar2(16),
     teacher_last_name    varchar2(16),
     class_id             varchar2(4),
     class_name           varchar2(40),
     constraint teacher_info_pk primary key (teacher_id)
     );
Table created.

SQL> insert into teacher_info (teacher_id, teacher_first_name,
     teacher_last_name, class_id, class_name)
```

```
    values (1001, 'Mohamed', 'Ibrahim', 'CS', 'Computer Science');
1 row created.

SQL> insert into teacher_info (teacher_id, teacher_first_name,
    teacher_last_name, class_id, class_name)
    values (1002, 'Mohamed', 'Yaseen', 'CS', 'Computer Science');
1 row created.

SQL> insert into teacher_info (teacher_id, teacher_first_name,
    teacher_last_name, class_id, class_name)
    values (1003, 'Karan', 'Singh', 'MGT', 'Management');
1 row created.

SQL> insert into teacher_info (teacher_id, teacher_first_name,
    teacher_last_name, class_id, class_name)
    values (1004, 'Kiran', 'Kumar', 'COM', 'Commerce');
1 row created.

SQL> insert into teacher_info (teacher_id, teacher_first_name,
    teacher_last_name, class_id, class_name)
    values (1005, 'Akhfa', 'Nafi', 'COM', 'Commerce');
1 row created.

SQL> insert into teacher_info (teacher_id, teacher_first_name,
    teacher_last_name, class_id, class_name)
    values (1006, 'Ravi', 'Chandren', 'MGT', 'Management');
1 row created.

SQL> insert into teacher_info (teacher_id, teacher_first_name,
    teacher_last_name, class_id, class_name)
    values (1007, 'Nitin', 'Otageri', 'ZOO', 'Zoology');
1 row created.

SQL> select * from teacher_info;
    TEACHER_ID TEACHER_FIRST_NA TEACHER_LAST_NAM CLAS CLASS_NAME
    ---------- ---------------- ---------------- ---- ----------------
          1001 Mohamed          Ibrahim          CS   Computer Science
          1002 Mohamed          Yaseen           CS   Computer Science
          1003 Karan            Singh            MGT  Management
          1004 Kiran            Kumar            COM  Commerce
          1005 Akhfa            Nafi             COM  Commerce
          1006 Ravi             Chandren         MGT  Management
          1007 Nitin            Otageri          ZOO  Zoology
7 rows selected.
```

In the above table, primary key is "teacher_id". As per normalization rule, every non-key filed should depend on primary key. So, we can insert a data as below:

```
SQL> insert into teacher_info (teacher_id, teacher_first_name,
     teacher_last_name, class_id, class_name)
     values (1008, 'Shahul', 'Hameed', 'COM', 'Computer Science');
1 row created.

SQL> insert into teacher_info (teacher_id, teacher_first_name,
     teacher_last_name, class_id, class_name)
     values (1009, 'Feroz', 'Khan', 'CS', 'Customer Service');
1 row created.

SQL> select * from teacher_info;
     TEACHER_ID TEACHER_FIRST_NA TEACHER_LAST_NAM CLAS CLASS_NAME
     ---------- ---------------- ---------------- ---- ----------------
           1001 Mohamed          Ibrahim          CS   Computer Science
           1002 Mohamed          Yaseen           CS   Computer Science
           1003 Karan            Singh            MGT  Management
           1004 Kiran            Kumar            COM  Commerce
           1005 Akhfa            Nafi             COM  Commerce
           1006 Ravi             Chandren         MGT  Management
           1007 Nitin            Otageri          ZOO  Zoology
           1008 Shahul           Hameed           COM  Computer Science
           1009 Feroz            Khan             CS   Customer Service
9 rows selected.
```

In our example, we are using department id "CS" to refer "Customer Service" and "COM" to refer "Commerce". But, in the above insertion, we used "CS" to refer "Customer Service" and "COM" to refer "Commerce". Here, we are loosing the "meaning" of data. We do not want these kinds of insertions.

The value in class_name is determined by the value in class_id, which is determined by the primary key value (teacher_id). Thus, the non-key field class_name becomes transitive dependent on primary key (teacher_id). We have to eliminate this transitive dependency in order to normalize the table compliant to third normal form, as below:

```
SQL> create table teacher
     ( teacher_id           number(4),
       teacher_first_name   varchar2(16),
       teacher_last_name    varchar2(16),
       class_id             varchar2(4) references class(class_id),
       constraint teacher_info_pk primary key (teacher_id)
     );
Table created.
```

```
SQL> create table class
     ( class_id    varchar2(4),
       class_name  varchar2(40),
       constraint class_pk primary key (class_id)
     );
Table created.

SQL> insert into class (class_id, class_name) values
     ('CS', 'Computer Science');
1 row created.

SQL> insert into class (class_id, class_name) values
     ('MGT', 'Management');
1 row created.

SQL> insert into class (class_id, class_name) values
     ('COM', 'Commerce');
1 row created.

SQL> insert into class (class_id, class_name) values
     ('ZOO', 'Zoology');
1 row created.

SQL> select * from class;
     CLAS   CLASS_NAME
     ----   -------------------
     CS     Computer Science
     MGT    Management
     COM    Commerce
     ZOO    Zoology

SQL> insert into teacher (teacher_id, teacher_first_name,
     teacher_last_name, class_id)
     values (1001, 'Mohamed', 'Ibrahim', 'CS');
1 row created.

SQL> insert into teacher (teacher_id, teacher_first_name,
     teacher_last_name, class_id)
     values (1002, 'Mohamed', 'Yaseen', 'CS');
1 row created.
```

```
SQL> insert into teacher (teacher_id, teacher_first_name,
     teacher_last_name, class_id)
     values (1003, 'Karan', 'Singh', 'MGT');
1 row created.

SQL> insert into teacher (teacher_id, teacher_first_name,
     teacher_last_name, class_id)
     values (1004, 'Kiran', 'Kumar', 'COM');
1 row created.

SQL> insert into teacher (teacher_id, teacher_first_name,
     teacher_last_name, class_id)
     values (1005, 'Akhfa', 'Nafi', 'COM');
1 row created.

SQL> insert into teacher (teacher_id, teacher_first_name,
     teacher_last_name, class_id)
     values (1006, 'Ravi', 'Chandren', 'MGT');
1 row created.

SQL> insert into teacher (teacher_id, teacher_first_name,
     teacher_last_name, class_id)
     values (1007, 'Nitin', 'Otageri', 'ZOO');
1 row created.

SQL> select * from teacher;
     TEACHER_ID TEACHER_FIRST_NA TEACHER_LAST_NAM  CLAS
     ---------- ---------------- ----------------  ----
           1001 Mohamed          Ibrahim           CS
           1002 Mohamed          Yaseen            CS
           1003 Karan            Singh             MGT
           1004 Kiran            Kumar             COM
           1005 Akhfa            Nafi              COM
           1006 Ravi             Chandren          MGT
           1007 Nitin            Otageri           ZOO
7 rows selected.
```

1.3.1.4 Boyce-Codd Normal Form (BCNF)

"A database table is in the Boyce-Codd Normal Form if it fulfils all the requirements of the third normal form and every determinant must be a candidate key."

Focus: If there are non-trivial dependencies between candidate key attributes, separate those attributes into distinct tables.

A relation schema **R** is in BCNF with respect to a set **F** of functional dependencies if for all functional dependencies in F^+ of the form $a \rightarrow b$, where **a** and **b** are the subsets of **R** ($a \subseteq b$ and $b \subseteq c$), at least one of the following holds:

- $a \rightarrow b$ is a trivial functional dependency ($b \subseteq a$)
- **a** is a super-key for **R.**

Functional dependency: An attribute **B** has a functional dependency on attribute **A** (**A** → **B**, **A** determines **B**) if, for each value of attribute **A**, there is exactly one value of attribute **B**. That is, the value in the column **B** is determined by the value in column **A**.

Trivial functional dependency: A trivial functional dependency is a functional dependency of an attribute on a superset of itself.

{loan_number, amount} → {loan_number} is trivial

A Functional Dependency is said to be Trivial Functional Dependency when the right hand side is contained within the left hand side (in set).

Super key: A set of attributes/an attribute which are/is able to identity any row in the database table is known as super key. There may be different set of attributes in a table to identify any row in the table (set of super keys). A minimal super key (a super key, with minimum number of attributes, among the set of super keys) is termed as candidate key. A candidate key has the designation to become a primary key; however the primary key is used to identify rows uniquely.

Example:

Consider a table (training) with three attributes (student, course, and teacher).

The business constraints are:

- Each student should take a given course from one teacher only.
- Each teacher should teach only one course.

Now, we define the table by assigning (*student, course*) as composite primary key as this composite primary key determines the value in *teacher* column.

(student, course) → teacher

```
SQL> create table training
     ( student  varchar2(16),
       course   varchar2(16),
       teacher  varchar2(16),
       constraint training_pk primary key (student, course)
     );
Table created.

SQL> insert into training (student, course, teacher) values
     ( 'Ibrahim', 'Java', 'John');
1 row created.

SQL> insert into training (student, course, teacher) values
     ( 'Ibrahim', 'Oracle', 'Karan');
1 row created.
```

```
SQL> insert into training (student, course, teacher) values
     ( 'Ibrahim', 'C++', 'Ahamed');
1 row created.

SQL> insert into training (student, course, teacher) values
     ( 'Akhfa', 'Java', 'John');
1 row created.

SQL> insert into training (student, course, teacher) values
     ( 'Akhfa', 'Oracle', 'Kumar');
1 row created.

SQL> insert into training (student, course, teacher) values
     ( 'Akhfa', 'C++', 'Karan');
1 row created.

SQL> select * from training;
     STUDENT             COURSE              TEACHER
     ----------------    ----------------    ----------------
     Ibrahim             Java                John
     Ibrahim             Oracle              Karan
     Ibrahim             C++                 Ahamed
     Akhfa               Java                John
     Akhfa               Oracle              Kumar
     Akhfa               C++                 Karan
6 rows selected.
```

The above table design confirms to third normal form. But, it fails to satisfy the business constraint — *"Each teacher should teach only one course"*. The last two rows of the above sample data show the failure this business rule.

The composite primary key (*student, course*) determines the value of *teacher*, but also the *teacher* determines *course*.

(student, course) → teacher

teacher → course

Observe that there is a overlapping of column *course*. The determinant (teacher → course) *teacher* which determines the value of the *course* is not the candidate key in our design. That is, the dependency *teacher* → *course* is a non-trivial functional dependency and *teacher* is not a super of the table. So, the design is not in BCNF.

Decompose the above table into two tables as below:

student_teacher (student, teacher)

teacher_course (teacher, course)

```
SQL> create table student_teacher
     ( student varchar2(16),
       teacher varchar2(16),
       constraint student_teacher_pk primary key (student, teacher)
     );
Table created.

SQL> insert into student_teacher (student, teacher) values
     ( 'Ibrahim', 'John');
1 row created.

SQL> insert into student_teacher (student, teacher) values
     ( 'Ibrahim', 'Karan');
1 row created.

SQL> insert into student_teacher (student, teacher) values
     ( 'Ibrahim', 'Ahamed');
1 row created.

SQL> insert into student_teacher (student, teacher) values
     ( 'Akhfa', 'John');
1 row created.

SQL> insert into student_teacher (student, teacher) values
     ( 'Akhfa', 'Kumar');
1 row created.

SQL> select * from  student_teacher;
     STUDENT            TEACHER
     ----------------   ----------------
     Akhfa              John
     Akhfa              Karan
     Akhfa              Kumar
     Ibrahim            Ahamed
     Ibrahim            John
     Ibrahim            Karan
6 rows selected.

SQL> create table teacher_course
     ( teacher varchar2(16),
       course  varchar2(16),
     constraint teacher_course_pk primary key (teacher, course)
     );
Table created.
```

```
SQL> insert into teacher_course (teacher, course) values
     ( 'John', 'Java');
1 row created.

SQL> insert into teacher_course (teacher, course) values
     ( 'Karan', 'Oracle');
1 row created.

SQL> insert into teacher_course (teacher, course) values
     ( 'Ahamed', 'C++');
1 row created.

SQL> insert into teacher_course (teacher, course) values
     ( 'Kumar', 'MySQL');
1 row created.

SQL> select * from  teacher_course;
     TEACHER              COURSE
     ----------------     ----------------
     Ahamed               C++
     John                 Java
     Karan                Oracle
     Kumar                MySQL
```

Now, the design confirms to BCNF. Note that this BCNF applies to situations when overlapping of candidate keys occurs. And if a table has no non-key fields, then it is automatically in BCNF.

1.3.1.5 Fourth Normal Form (4NF)

"A database table is in the forth normal form if it fulfils all the requirements of the Boyce-Codd normal form and it should not contain more than one independent multi-valued dependencies."

Focus: Eliminate two or more unrelated (not directly related) one-to-many (`1:m`) or many-to-many (`n:m`) relationships in a table, create a table for each relationship.

A relation schema **R** is in Forth Normal Form if, for every one of its non-trivial multi-valued dependencies **a** $\twoheadrightarrow$ **b**, **a** is a super-key.

Multi-valued dependency: A Functional Dependency **a** $\rightarrow$ **b** relates one value of a to one value of **b**. A multi-valued dependency **a** $\twoheadrightarrow$ **b** relates one value of a to **a** set of values of **b**.

A non-trivial multi-valued dependency occurs only when the table contains at least three attributes and two of them are multi-valued. For example, assume a table contains three attributes (**a**, **b**, **c**), for each value in attribute **a**, there is a set of values for attribute **b** and a set of values for attribute **c**, but the attributes **b** and **c** are not related (independent).

Example:

```
SQL> create table skill
     ( employee         varchar2(16),
       software_skill   varchar2(16),
```

```
        spoken_language varchar2(16),
        constraint skill_pk primary key
                (employee, software_skill, spoken_language)
    );
Table created.

SQL> insert into skill (employee, software_skill, spoken_language)
     values ('Ibrahim', 'Java', 'English');
1 row created.

SQL> insert into skill (employee, software_skill, spoken_language)
     values ('Ibrahim', 'C++', 'English');
1 row created.

SQL> insert into skill (employee, software_skill, spoken_language)
     values ('Ibrahim', 'Java', 'Tamil');
1 row created.

SQL> insert into skill (employee, software_skill, spoken_language)
     values ('Ibrahim', 'C++', 'Tamil');
1 row created.

SQL> insert into skill (employee, software_skill, spoken_language)
     values ('Karan', 'Oracle', 'Hindi');
1 row created.

SQL> insert into skill (employee, software_skill, spoken_language)
     values ('Karan', 'C++', 'Hindi');
1 row created.

SQL> select * from skill;
     EMPLOYEE            SOFTWARE_SKILL      SPOKEN_LANGUAGE
     ----------------    ----------------    ----------------
     Ibrahim             C++                 English
     Ibrahim             C++                 Tamil
     Ibrahim             Java                English
     Ibrahim             Java                Tamil
     Karan               C++                 Hindi
     Karan               Oracle              Hindi
6 rows selected.
```

An Employee can know more than one software and more than one spoken language. A software product can be known by many employees, and also a spoken language can be known by many employees.

A primary key for the above table design is a composite primary key of all three attributes. Now, the table is in BCNF. But, there are two multi-valued independent dependencies occurred.

Two multi-valued dependencies are,

employee $\rightarrow\!\!\!\rightarrow$ software_skill (many to many relationship)

employee $\rightarrow\!\!\!\rightarrow$ spoken_language (many to many relationship)

But, the attributes *software_skill* and *spoken_language* are not logically related. So, decompose the table as shown below in order to confirm to forth normal form.

```
SQL> create table employee_software
     ( employee       varchar2(16),
       software_skill varchar2(16),
       constraint employee_software_pk primary key
                        (employee, software_skill)
     );
Table created.

SQL> create table employee_language
     ( employee        varchar2(16),
       spoken_language varchar2(16),
       constraint employee_language_pk primary key
                        (employee, spoken_language)
     );
Table created.

SQL> insert into employee_software (employee, software_skill) values
     ( 'Ibrahim', 'Java');
1 row created.

SQL> insert into employee_software (employee, software_skill) values
     ( 'Ibrahim', 'C++');
1 row created.

SQL> insert into employee_software (employee, software_skill) values
     ( 'Karan', 'Oracle');
1 row created.

SQL> insert into employee_software (employee, software_skill) values
     ( 'Karan', 'C++');
1 row created.

SQL> insert into employee_language (employee, spoken_language) values
     ( 'Ibrahim', 'English');
1 row created.
```

```
SQL> insert into employee_language (employee, spoken_language) values
     ( 'Ibrahim', 'Tamil');
1 row created.

SQL> insert into employee_language (employee, spoken_language) values
     ( 'Karan', 'Hindi');
1 row created.

SQL> select * from employee_software;
     EMPLOYEE            SOFTWARE_SKILL
     ----------------    ----------------
     Ibrahim             C++
     Ibrahim             Java
     Karan               C++
     Karan               Oracle

SQL> select * from employee_language;
     EMPLOYEE            SPOKEN_LANGUAGE
     ----------------    ----------------
     Ibrahim             English
     Ibrahim             Tamil
     Karan               Hindi

SQL> select t1.employee, t1.software_skill, t2.spoken_language from
     employee_software t1, employee_language t2
     where t1.employee = t2.employee;
     EMPLOYEE            SOFTWARE_SKILL      SPOKEN_LANGUAGE
     ----------------    ----------------    ----------------
     Ibrahim             C++                 Tamil
     Ibrahim             C++                 English
     Ibrahim             Java                Tamil
     Ibrahim             Java                English
     Karan               C++                 Hindi
     Karan               Oracle              Hindi
6 rows selected.
```

1.3.1.6 Fifth Normal Form (5NF)

"A database table is in the fifth normal form, also called as Projection-Join normal form, if it fulfils all the requirements of the forth normal form and the table's every join dependency is implied by the candidate keys."

Focus: Reduce redundancy of data which are not eliminated by first to fourth normal forms, by isolating semantically (logically) related relationships.

Join Dependency: A relation R satisfies join dependency **(R1, R2, ..., Rn)** if and only if **R** is equal to the join of **R1, R2, ..., Rn** where **Ri** are subsets of the set of attributes of **R**. That is, if a table is decomposed into several tables, then joining of those tables should make the original table without any loss of data integrity and conflicts.

Projection-Join: A Projection is a table (decomposed part of decomposable table), which contains a subset of fields from an original table. Joining all projected tables give original table.

Example:

Consider a table stud_dep_sub with three attributes (student, department, subject).

```
SQL> create table stud_dep_sub
     ( student      varchar2(16),
       department   varchar2(32),
       subject      varchar2(16),
       constraint stud_dep_sub_pk primary key
                    (student, department, subject)
     );
Table created.

SQL> insert into stud_dep_sub (student, department, subject) values
     ( 'Ibrahim', 'Computer Science', 'Java');
1 row created.

SQL> insert into stud_dep_sub (student, department, subject) values
     ( 'Ibrahim', 'Management', 'Marketing');
1 row created.

SQL> insert into stud_dep_sub (student, department, subject) values
     ( 'Karan', 'Computer Science', 'Oracle');
1 row created.

SQL> insert into stud_dep_sub (student, department, subject) values
     ( 'Ajay', 'Computer Science', 'C++');
1 row created.

SQL> insert into stud_dep_sub (student, department, subject) values
     ( 'Nitin', 'Chemistry', 'Bio-Chemistry');
1 row created.

SQL> insert into stud_dep_sub (student, department, subject) values
     ( 'Nitin', 'Management', 'Marketing');
1 row created.
```

```
SQL> select * from stud_dep_sub;
     STUDENT          DEPARTMENT                  SUBJECT
     ---------------- --------------------------- ----------------
     Ajay             Computer Science            C++
     Ibrahim          Computer Science            Java
     Ibrahim          Management                  Marketing
     Karan            Computer Science            Oracle
     Nitin            Chemistry                   Bio-Chemistry
     Nitin            Management                  Marketing
6 rows selected.
```

All the three attributes form a composite primary key on the table. For each student entry, we have to insert values for department and subject. It is the same case for insertion of data for other attributes. This results in data duplication. The first four normal forms will not eliminate this kind of duplicate data. The fifth normal form attempts to eliminate duplication on this type of design.

The current design is as below:

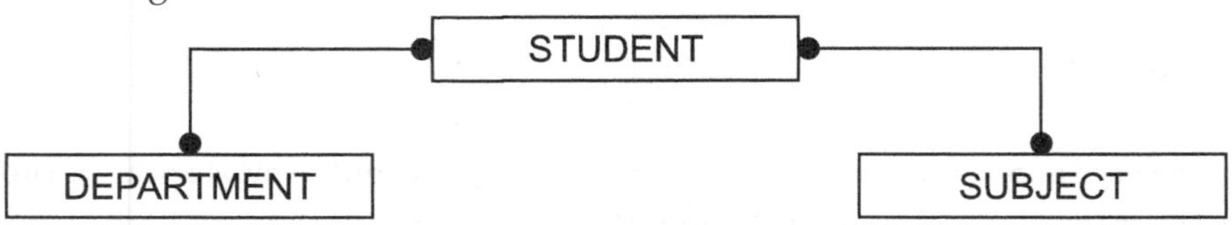

We can decompose the above table as below.

stud_dep (student, department)

stud_sub (student, subject)

```
SQL> create table stud_dep
     ( student varchar2(16),
       department     varchar2(32),
       constraint stud_dep_pk primary key (student, department)
     );
Table created.

SQL> insert into stud_dep (student, department) values
     ( 'Ajay', 'Computer Science');
1 row created.

SQL> insert into stud_dep (student, department) values
     ( 'Ibrahim', 'Computer Science');
1 row created.

SQL> insert into stud_dep (student, department) values
     ( 'Ibrahim', 'Management');
1 row created.
```

```
SQL> insert into stud_dep (student, department) values
     ( 'Karan', 'Computer Science');
1 row created.

SQL> insert into stud_dep (student, department) values
     ( 'Nitin', 'Chemistry');
1 row created.

SQL> insert into stud_dep (student, department) values
     ( 'Nitin', 'Management');
1 row created.

SQL> create table stud_sub
     ( student   varchar2(16),
       subject   varchar2(16),
       constraint stud_sub_pk primary key (student, subject)
     );
Table created.

SQL> insert into stud_sub (student, subject) values
     ( 'Ajay', 'C++');
1 row created.

SQL> insert into stud_sub (student, subject) values
     ( 'Ibrahim', 'Java');
1 row created.

SQL> insert into stud_sub (student, subject) values
     ( 'Ibrahim', 'Marketing');
1 row created.

SQL> insert into stud_sub (student, subject) values
     ( 'Karan', 'Oracle');
1 row created.

SQL> insert into stud_sub (student, subject) values
     ( 'Nitin', 'Bio-Chemistry');
1 row created.

SQL> insert into stud_sub (student, subject) values
     ( 'Nitin', 'Marketing');
1 row created.
```

```
SQL> select * from stud_dep;
     STUDENT             DEPARTMENT
     ----------------    --------------------------------
     Ajay                Computer Science
     Ibrahim             Computer Science
     Ibrahim             Management
     Karan               Computer Science
     Nitin               Chemistry
     Nitin               Management
6 rows selected.

SQL> select * from stud_sub;
     STUDENT             SUBJECT
     ----------------    ----------------
     Ajay                C++
     Ibrahim             Java
     Ibrahim             Marketing
     Karan               Oracle
     Nitin               Bio-Chemistry
     Nitin               Marketing
6 rows selected.
```

Joining these two tables should result the original table. But, in our case, unexpected result occurred as shown below:

```
SQL> select t1.student, t1.department, t2.subject from
     stud_dep t1, stud_sub t2 where t1.student = t2.student;
     STUDENT             DEPARTMENT                 SUBJECT
     ----------------    -----------------------    ----------------
     Ajay                Computer Science           C++
     Ibrahim             Computer Science           Java
     Ibrahim             Computer Science           Marketing
     Ibrahim             Management                 Java
     Ibrahim             Management                 Marketing
     Karan               Computer Science           Oracle
     Nitin               Chemistry                  Bio-Chemistry
     Nitin               Chemistry                  Marketing
     Nitin               Management                 Bio-Chemistry
     Nitin               Management                 Marketing
10 rows selected.

SQL> select * from stud_dep_sub;
     STUDENT             DEPARTMENT                 SUBJECT
     ----------------    ----------------------     ----------------
     Ajay                Computer Science           C++
     Ibrahim             Computer Science           Java
```

```
    Ibrahim         Management          Marketing
    Karan           Computer Science    Oracle
    Nitin           Chemistry           Bio-Chemistry
    Nitin           Management          Marketing
6 rows selected.
```

Joining of two table results in 10 rows, whereas original table contains only 6 rows. And also the result of join produces invalid data (for example, *Computer Science* department is linked with *Marketing* subject).

A cyclic dependency occurred in the original table, as (student, department, subject) forms a composite primary key for the table and the values in these fields are related in pairs of (student, department), (department, subject) and (student, subject). The fifth normal form focuses on completely removing this kind of cyclic redundancies in a table.

The design of our relation should be as below:

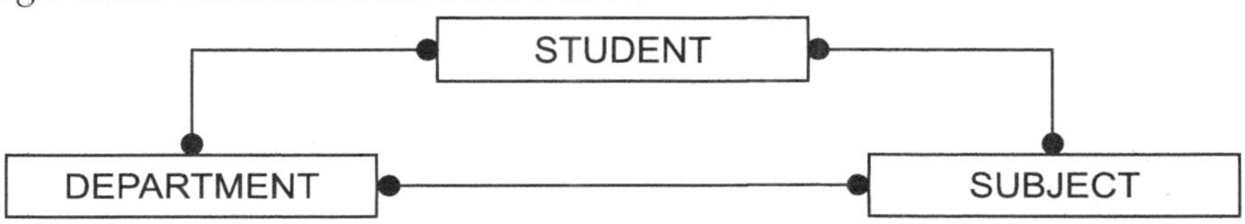

We already decompose the original table *stud_dep_sub (student, department, subject)* into *stud_dep (student, department)* and *stud_sub (student, subject)*. Now, create a new table which relates *department* and *subject* as shown below:

```
dept_sub (department, subject)
SQL> create table dept_sub
     ( department  varchar2(32),
       subject     varchar2(16),
       constraint dept_sub_pk primary key (department, subject)
     );
Table created.

SQL> insert into dept_sub (department, subject) values
     ( 'Computer Science', 'Java');
1 row created.

SQL> insert into dept_sub (department, subject) values
     ( 'Computer Science', 'C++');
1 row created.

SQL> insert into dept_sub (department, subject) values
     ( 'Computer Science', 'Oracle');
1 row created.

SQL> insert into dept_sub (department, subject) values
     ( 'Management', 'Marketing');
1 row created.
```

```
SQL> insert into dept_sub (department, subject) values
     ( 'Chemistry', 'Bio-Chemistry');
1 row created.

SQL> select * from dept_sub;
     DEPARTMENT                 SUBJECT
     -----------------------    ----------------
     Chemistry                  Bio-Chemistry
     Computer Science           C++
     Computer Science           Java
     Computer Science           Oracle
     Management                 Marketing
```

Joining of these tables forms the original table without loss of any data and integrity of data also remained.

```
SQL> select t1.student, t1.department, t2.subject from
     stud_dep t1, stud_sub t2, dept_sub t3 where
     t1.student = t2.student and t2.subject = t3.subject
     and t1.department = t3.department;
     STUDENT          DEPARTMENT              SUBJECT
     ---------------- -------------------     ----------------
     Nitin            Chemistry               Bio-Chemistry
     Ajay             Computer Science        C++
     Ibrahim          Computer Science        Java
     Karan            Computer Science        Oracle
     Ibrahim          Management              Marketing
     Nitin            Management              Marketing
6 rows selected.

SQL> select * from stud_dep_sub;
     STUDENT          DEPARTMENT              SUBJECT
     ---------------- ------------------------ ----------------
     Ajay             Computer Science        C++
     Ibrahim          Computer Science        Java
     Ibrahim          Management              Marketing
     Karan            Computer Science        Oracle
     Nitin            Chemistry               Bio-Chemistry
     Nitin            Management              Marketing
6 rows selected.
```

A core benefit of fifth normal form: Assume that there are 1000 students, 50 departments, and 200 subjects. If we choose the original table design,

stud_dep_sub (student, department, subject)

then, there will be 10,000,000 (1000 * 50 * 200) potential records.

If we choose the design after applying fifth normal form,

stud_dep (student, department)

stud_sub (student, subject)

dept_sub (department, subject)

there will be 50,000 (1000 * 50) potential records from *stud_dep* table,

there will be 200,000 (1000 * 200) potential records from *stud_sub* table, and

there will be 10,000 (50 * 200) potential records from *dept_sub* table.

So that, at most 260,000 records in this design.

Observe that the table before fifth normal form is applies requires storage for 10,000,000 records (at most), but the storage for only 260,000 records is required (at most) if we apply fifth normal form. That is how, the fifth normal form eliminates duplicate of data that those duplicates are not eliminated by first to forth normal forms.

1.3.2 De-normalization

One of the major goals of Normalization is to eliminate redundant of data. However, if a table decomposed into several table due to normalization, then a query on the data will take more CPU time as it has to join tables.

De-normalization is a technique to move from higher to lower normal forms of database modeling in order to speed up database operations. This De-normalization process allows redundant data in database table design to get rid of complex join, in order to optimize database performance.

Higher normalization slows down the database access, higher de-normalization (lower normalization) makes worst in maintaining redundant data. Which one to take? Apply normal forms according to the nature and accessibility of data. Majority of database community suggest that it is significant to apply normalization up to third normal form.

SUMMARY

This chapter started with introduction to RDBMS, and briefly explained the importance of database keys. Finally this chapter explored the necessary of database normalization with several normal forms.

Chapter 2

WORKING WITH ORACLE DATABASE

2.0 INTRODUCTION

Oracle is one of the most used Relational Database Management System (RDBMS) in industries. This chapter gives you a quick overview of SQL and PL/SQL to work with Oracle.

2.1 INSTALLING ORACLE

The "Oracle" software is a product from Oracle Corporation, can also be downloaded from Oracle's official website, *http://otn.oracle.com* for evaluation. You can download the free version of this software, but storage of data is limited (up to only 4 GB) and you have to follow licensing agreement. The letter '*g*' in the version number (10g) represents grid.

2.1.1 Installation Procedure for MS Windows

Insert the Oracle 10g CD in CD-Drive (If the software is stored on CD-ROM) and let *Autorun* to run. A window titled "Oracle Database 10g – Autorun" will be displayed with three options. Click on "Install/Deinstall Products" option. If you have software on Hard Disk, or any other storage medium that *Autorun* feature is not supported, then click on "setup.exe" file to start installation.

A window titled "Oracle Database 10g Installation" will be displayed. Keep the default values. And put a password for super-user in 'Database Password' textbox and confirm the same in 'Confirm Password' textbox. I am setting the password as 'ibrahim' (Please make a note the password that you entered, because it is required for administration purposes, for example for creating new user). Then, click on 'Next' button.

A window titled "Oracle Universal Installer: Summary" will be displayed. Click on 'Install' button. Then, installation process will be started. It will take several minutes. Wait until it finishes installation. After the installation is completed, the following window will be displayed. Click on 'Exit' button.

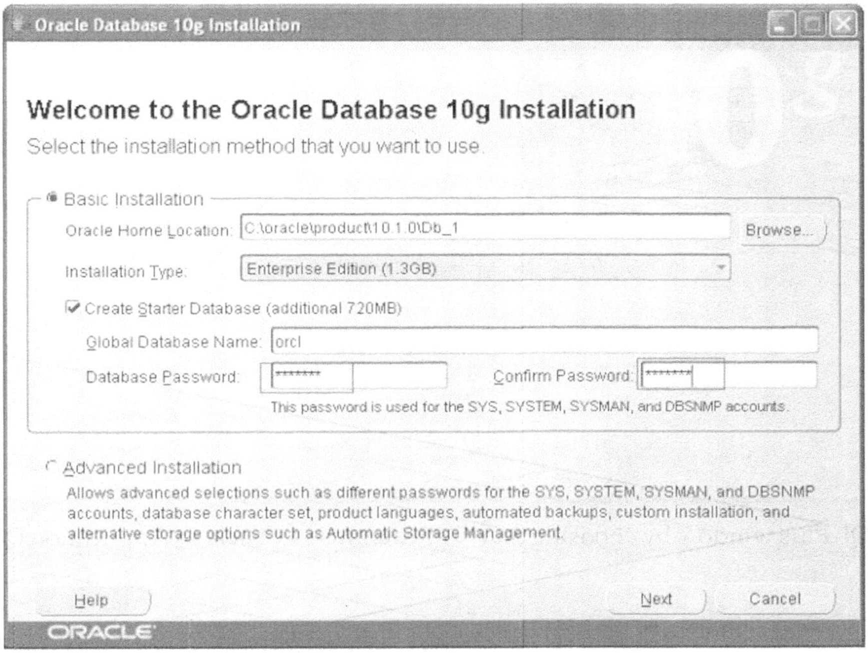

The end of Oracle Installation will be appeared as shown below.

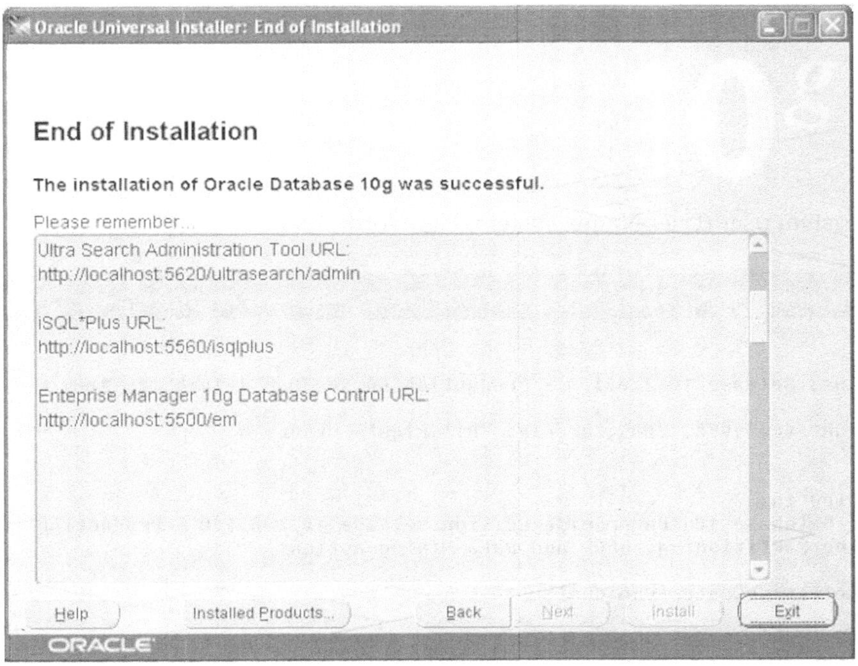

Testing oracle installation:

Start Oracle services (Invoke Service window through Control Panel, and start required Oracle services).

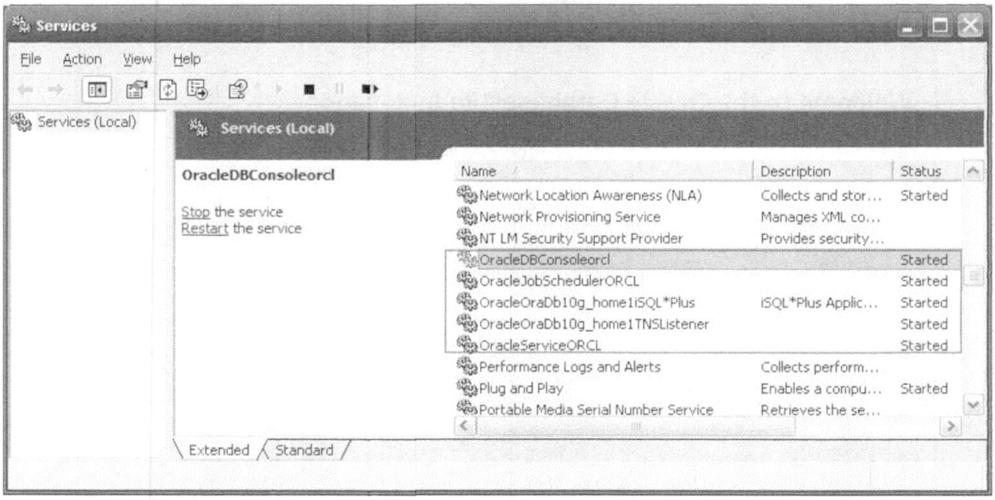

Invoke SQL Plus window by choosing Start → Programs → Oracle → Application Development → SQL Plus

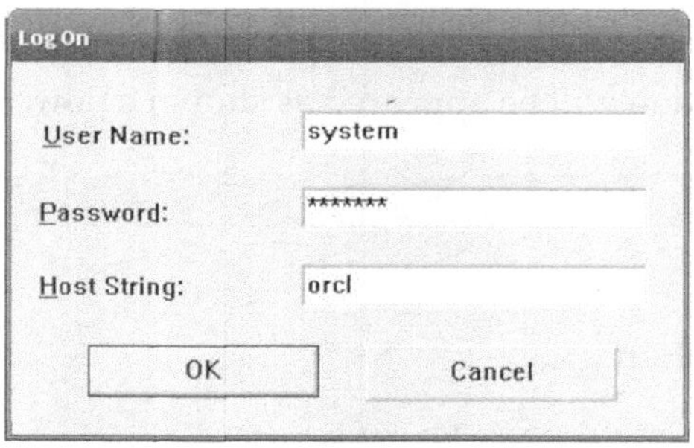

Login as system user (User Name: system, Password: ibrahim, Host String: orcl).

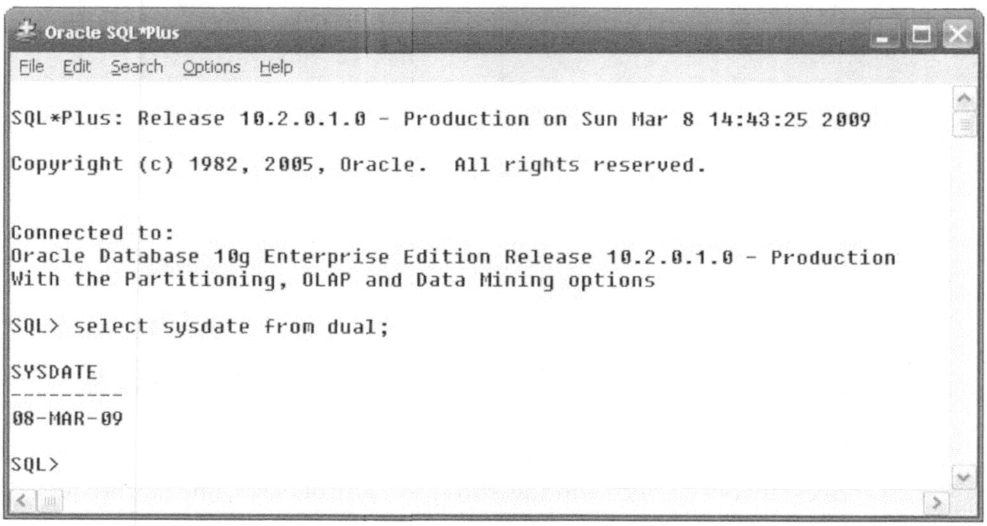

You can also use Oracle Client Tools, such as SQL Developer, DB Visualizer, and Aqua Data Studio, to access Oracle from local/remote machines.

2.2 ADDING/DELETING A USER

Oracle 10g also supports web-based interface for administering and maintaining database, along with the traditional way (commands at SQL prompt).

Adding/deleting a user via GUI interface:

Open a browser with address http://localhost:5500/em.

Note: Use the displayed URL while installing Oracle. Otherwise, you can invoke this web-based Enterprise Manger through Start → Programs → Oracle → Database Control menu items.

A page will be displayed like below (Web based Oracle Enterprise Manager).

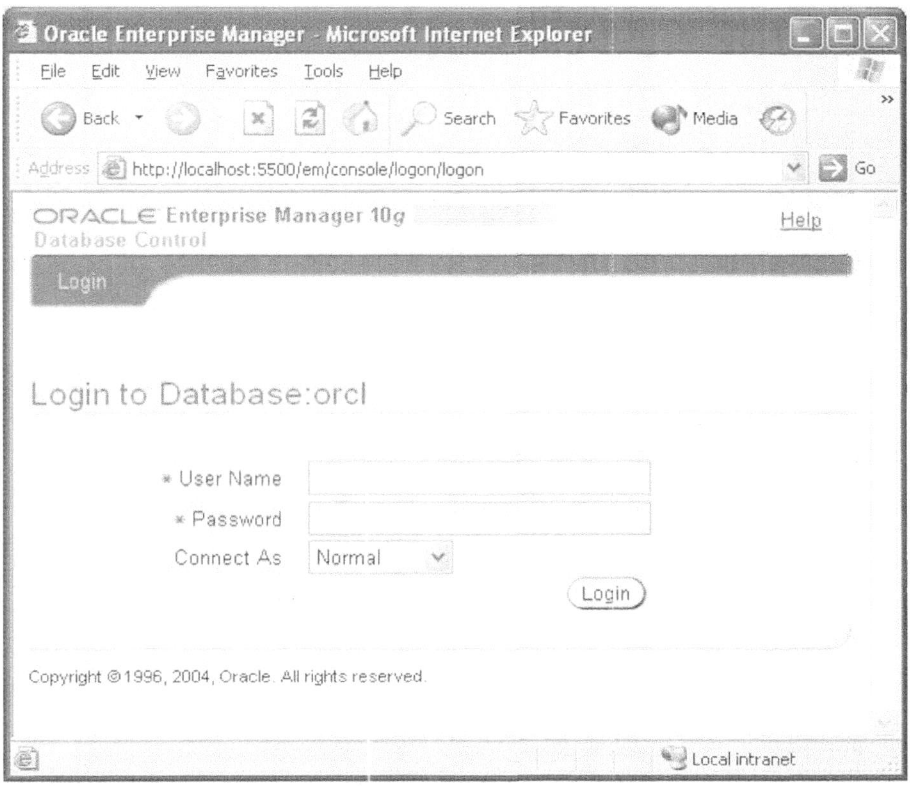

Enter 'system' as User Name and 'ibrahim' (specified as system administrator password at the installation process. Note that I specified ibrahim as password) as Password, and click "Login" button.

Then, a new page will be displayed as shown below. (This page may vary to versions).

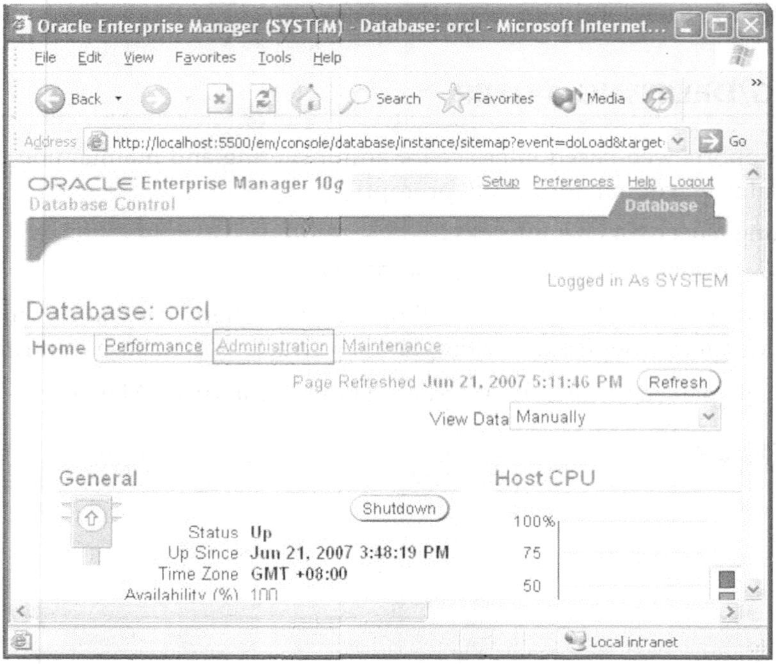

Click the "Administration" link. Then you will get the following page.

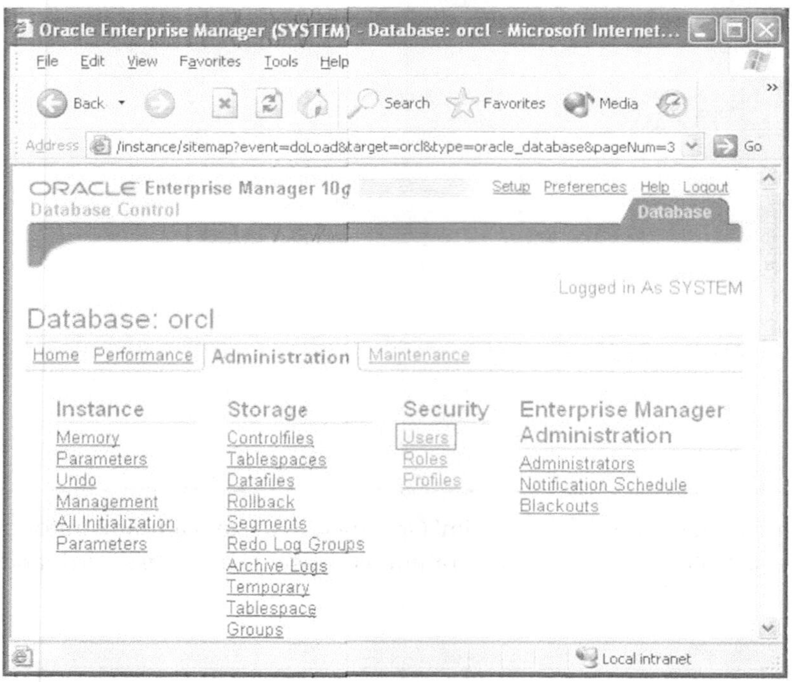

Click the "Users" link. Then, you will get a User Management screen with list of users as default display. Here, you can create, delete, set/reset privileges for a user.

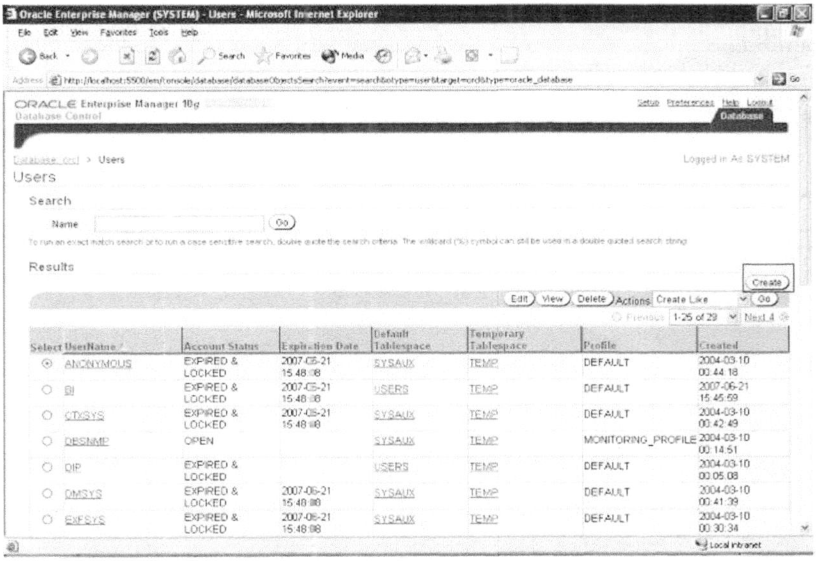

Click on the 'Create' button.

In the resultant page, enter the required information and click on "OK" button. Then, the user will be created.

If you want to follow our example, enter 'user1' in Name text field, 'user1' as Password and confirm the same. Click on the *Torch Light* button nearer to Default Tablespace. Then you will get a pop-up window.

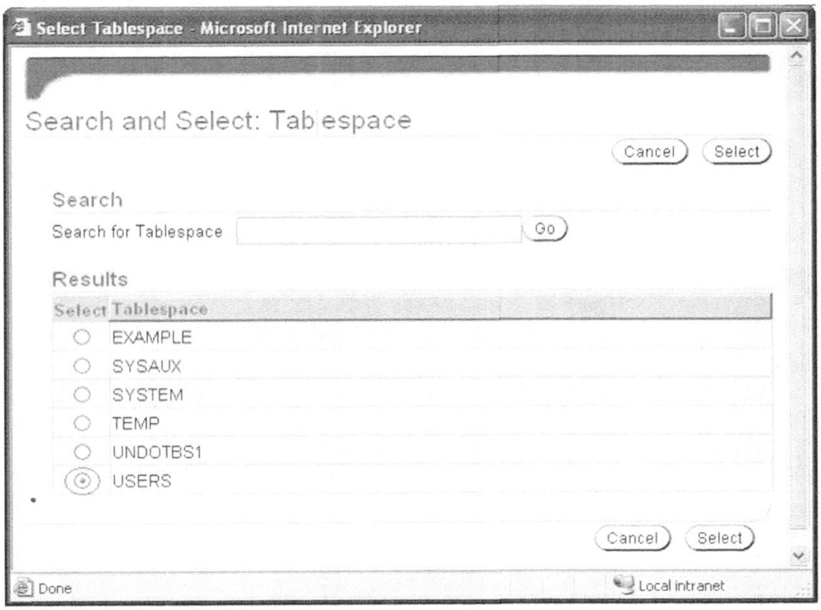

Select USERS radio button and click on "Select" button.

Click on "Roles" tab link in the main window.

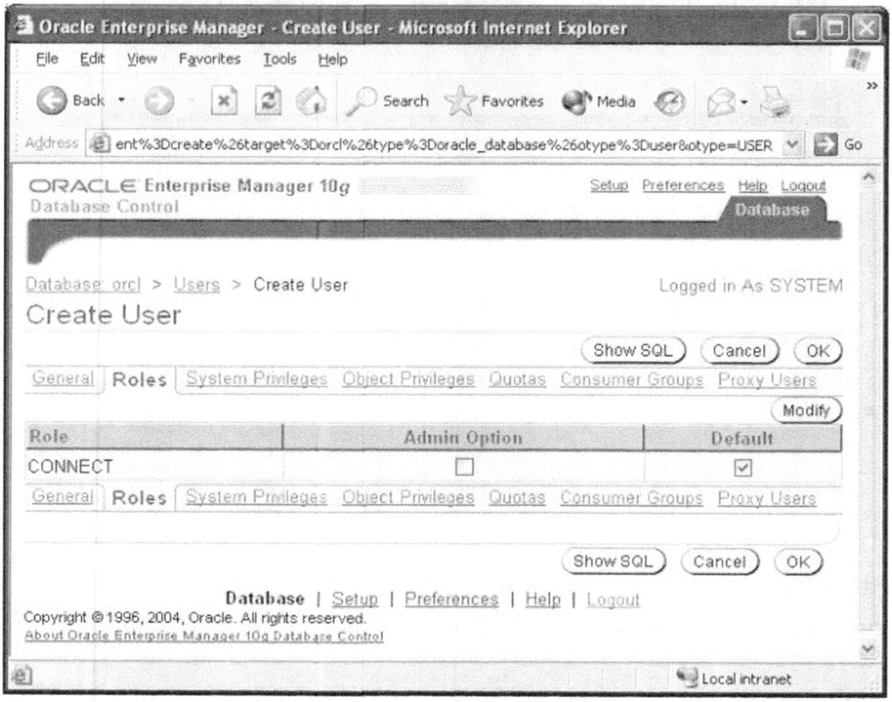

Click on "Modify" button. A pop-up window will be opened.

Move "RESOURCE" item from Available Roles List box to Selected Roles List box. Make sure that the Selected Roles List already contains "CONNECT" item. Now the Selected Roles List box contains two items: CONNECT and RESOURCES. Click on "OK" button.

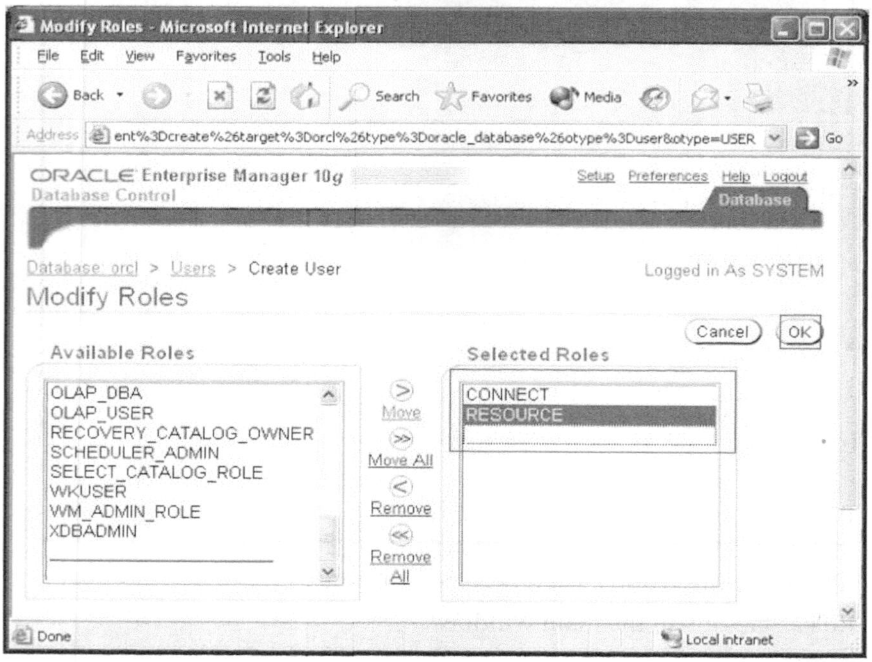

Then, make sure that Default check boxes are checked and click "OK" button on the invoked window.

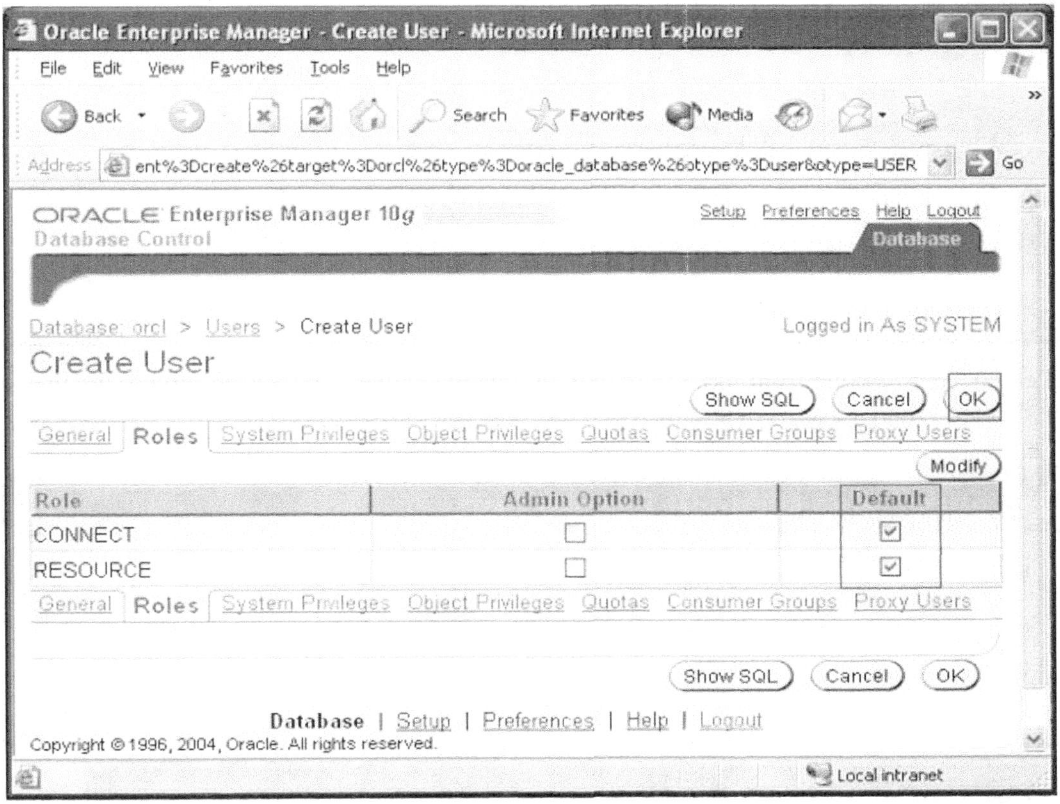

Then, you can see the added user in the list.

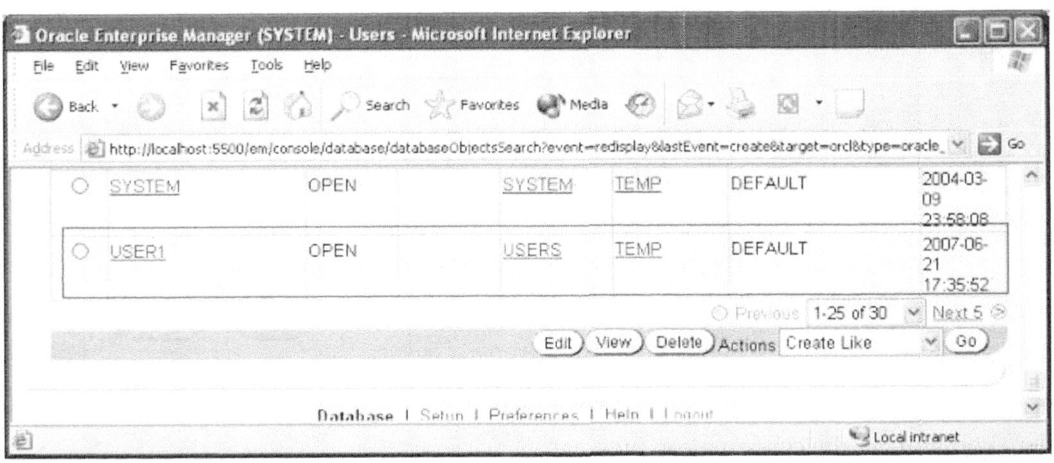

To delete a user, select the corresponding radio button and click on "Delete" button. To delete the user "USER1", select the user and click on "Delete" button.

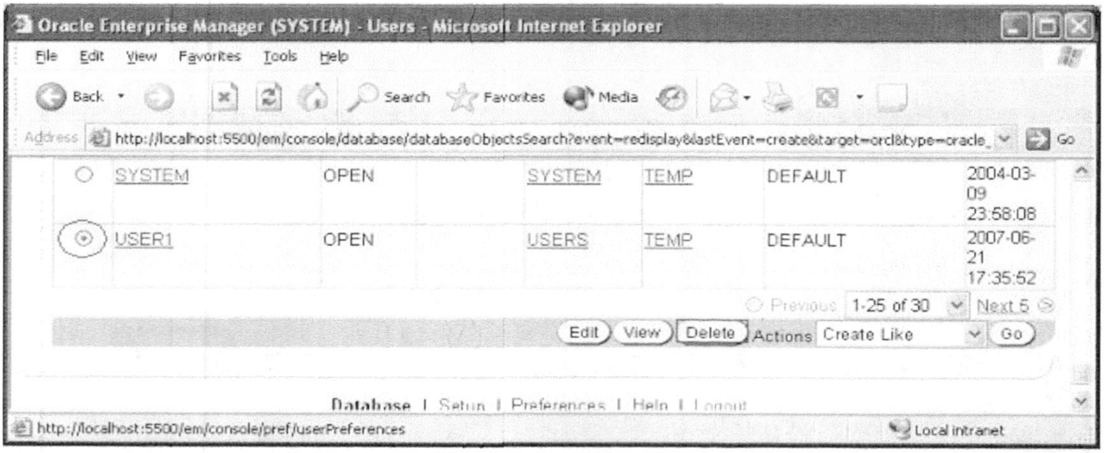

Click on "Yes" while prompted. (Note that all the tables/views/data pertaining to the user also will be deleted when a user is deleted.)

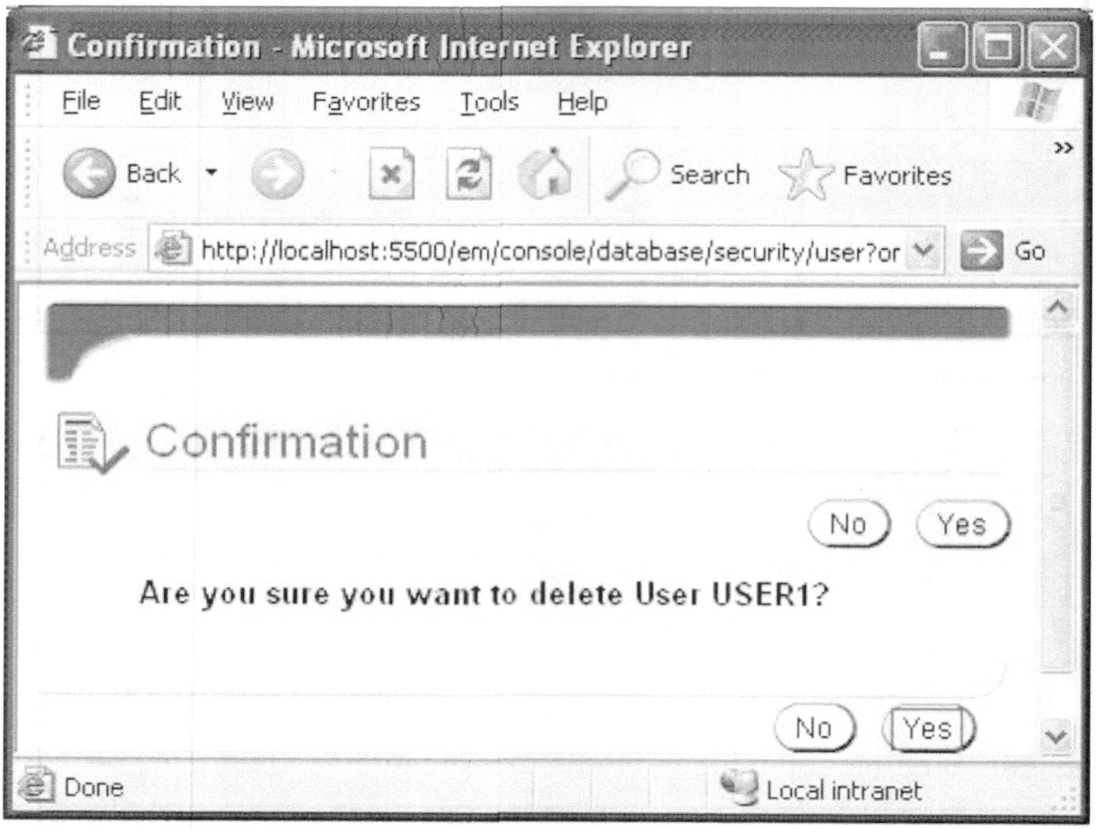

Then, you will get the confirmation message.

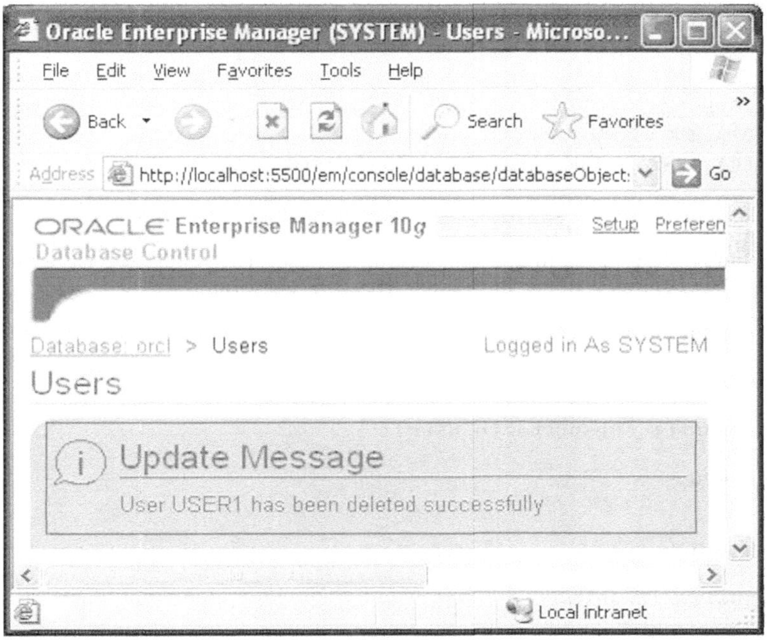

Adding/deleting a user via SQL commands:

Invoke SQL Plus window (by choosing Start → Programs → Oracle → Application Development → SQL Plus) and login as "system" user.

[User Name: system, Password: Ibrahim (for example), Host String: orcl].

Note: You can use any Oracle client also.

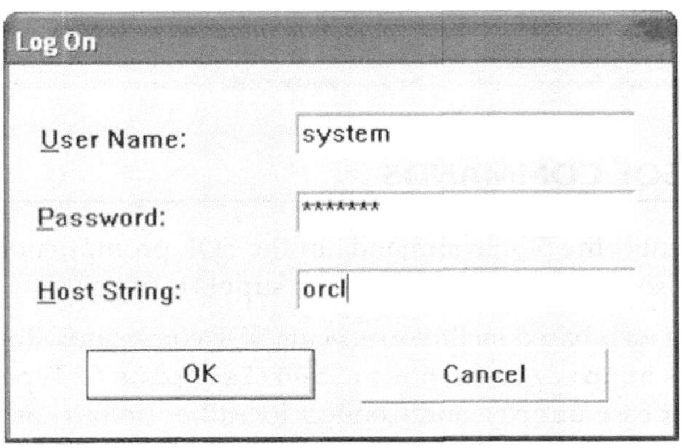

Then, you will get the SQL window (logged as "system" user). Enter the following commands to create a user 'user1' with password 'user1'.

```
create user user1 identified by user1 default tablespace USERS;
grant connect, resource to user1;
```

You can also login to 'user1' on this same window by using the command `'conn username/password'`, in our case `'conn user1/user1'`.

To drop the user 'user1', use the following command in Administrator (system) account.

```
Oracle SQL*Plus
File Edit Search Options Help
Copyright (c) 1982, 2004, Oracle.  All rights reserved.


Connected to:
Oracle Database 10g Enterprise Edition Release 10.1.0.2.0 - Production
With the Partitioning, OLAP and Data Mining options

SQL> create user user1 identified by user1 default tablespace USERS;

User created.

SQL> grant connect, resource to user1;

Grant succeeded.

SQL>
SQL> conn user1/user1
Connected.
SQL> conn system/ibrahim
Connected.
SQL> drop user user1 cascade;

User dropped.

SQL> conn user1/user1
ERROR:
ORA-01017: invalid username/password; logon denied


Warning: You are no longer connected to ORACLE.
SQL> |
```

2.3 EXECUTING SQL COMMANDS

Open SQL prompt and enter the SQL commands in the SQL prompt ended with semi-colon (as shown above). You can also use any SQL client which supports Oracle.

Oracle 10g provides a web-based facility to execute SQL commands. To use this facility, invoke any browser with address `http://localhost:5560/isqlplus/`. Type Username (in our case `user1`), Password (in our case `user1`), and Connect Identifier (in our case `orcl`) and then press "Login" button.

Type the SQL command in the specified Text Area and press "Execute" button.

For example, I am here creating a table named "test1".

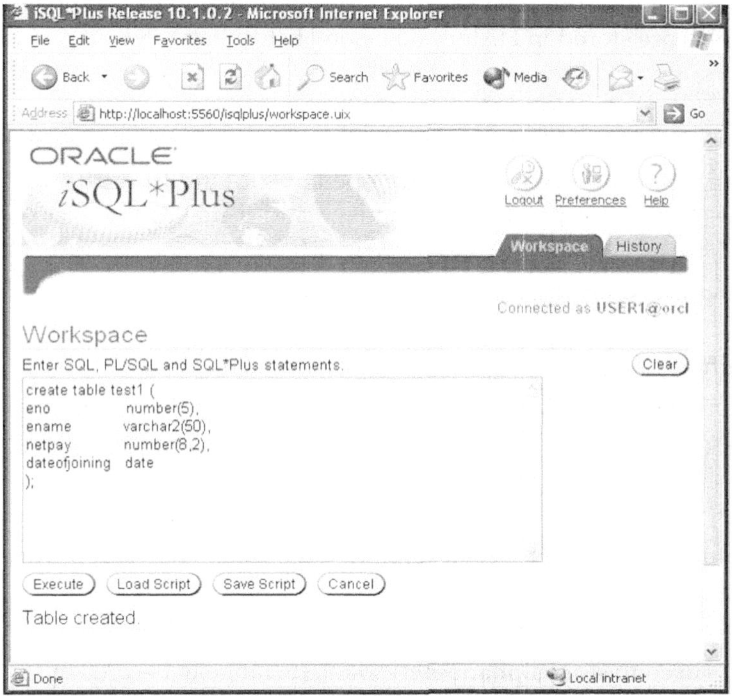
iSQL*Plus Release 10.1.0.2 - Microsoft Internet Explorer
File Edit View Favorites Tools Help
Back Search Favorites Media
Address http://localhost:5560/isqlplus/workspace.uix Go
ORACLE
iSQL*Plus
Logout Preferences Help
Workspace History
Connected as USER1@orcl
Workspace
Enter SQL, PL/SQL and SQL*Plus statements.
Clear
create table test1 (
eno number(5),
ename varchar2(50),
netpay number(8,2),
dateofjoining date
);
Execute Load Script Save Script Cancel
Table created.
Done
Local intranet

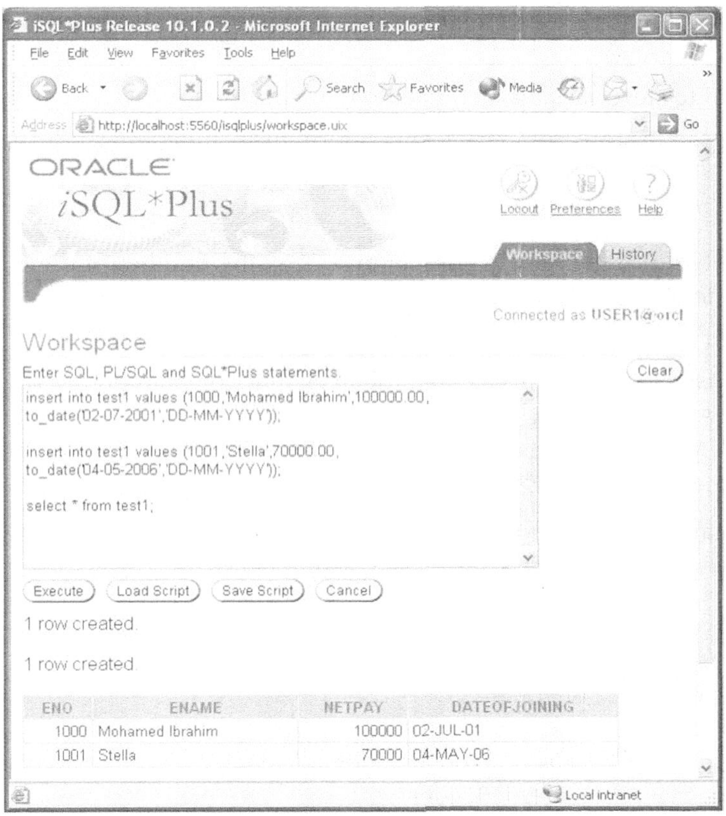
iSQL*Plus Release 10.1.0.2 - Microsoft Internet Explorer
File Edit View Favorites Tools Help
Back Search Favorites Media
Address http://localhost:5560/isqlplus/workspace.uix Go
ORACLE
iSQL*Plus
Logout Preferences Help
Workspace History
Connected as USER1@orcl
Workspace
Enter SQL, PL/SQL and SQL*Plus statements.
Clear
insert into test1 values (1000,'Mohamed Ibrahim',100000.00,
to_date('02-07-2001','DD-MM-YYYY'));
insert into test1 values (1001,'Stella',70000.00,
to_date('04-05-2006','DD-MM-YYYY'));
select * from test1;
Execute Load Script Save Script Cancel
1 row created.
1 row created.
ENO ENAME NETPAY DATEOFJOINING
1000 Mohamed Ibrahim 100000 02-JUL-01
1001 Stella 70000 04-MAY-06
Local intranet

Another advantage of user this web-based interface is that you can access the previously used SQL commands, which are stored in History (click on History tab to view).

2.4 SQL

The Structured Query Language (SQL) was developed by IBM in early 1970's and it is the database language for Oracle. It is a non-procedural language and it makes the user to interact with the database.

The SQL provides the following three types of commands to the user to communicate with the database.

- Data Definition Language (DDL) : create, alter, drop
- Data Manipulation Language (DML) : select, insert, delete, update
- Transaction Control Language (TCL) : commit, savepoint, rollback

2.4.1 Data Types

A data type should be specified for each column of the table. The SQL allows the following data types.

`char` : It is used to store alphanumeric data. Its range is 1 – 255 bytes.

`varchar2` : It is used to store alphanumeric data. Its range is 1 – 2000 bytes. If the user enters a value that is shorter than the specified length, then the database would blank-pad to the fixed length in *char* datatype, but in *varchar2* datatype, the column's length is assumed as the user entered datum's length.

`long` : It is used to store variable character length data.

`number` : It is used to store numbers. General formats include,

number(d)

number(d,f)

were, 'd' is the number of digits in the number and 'f' is the number of digits after the decimal point in the case of floating point numbers.

`date` : It is used to store dates. (The default date type is dd-mon-yy).

`raw`(size) : It is used to store byte oriented (binary) data (for example, storing images).

`long raw` : It is used to store variable length binary data.

2.4.2 DDL Commands

The DDL commands are used to do data definition operation such as creation of new tables, altering the structure of existing tables and drop existing tables.

2.4.2.1 create

This command creates a table.

General format:

```
create table <table-name> (column-name1 datatype, column-name2 datatype,
                           ...)
```

Example

```
SQL> create table student (rno number(5), sname varchar2(15),
                                m1 number(3), m2 number(3) );
```

Table created.

2.4.2.2 *alter*

The alter command alters the structure of an existing table.

General format:

```
alter table <table-name> add (column-name datatype, column-name datatype,
                                ...)
alter table <table-name> modify (column-name datatype, column-name datatype,
                                ...)
```

Example:

```
SQL> desc student;
    Name                              Null?     Type
    -------------------------------   --------  ----
    RNO                                         NUMBER(5)
    SNAME                                       VARCHAR2(15)
    M1                                          NUMBER(3)
    M2                                          NUMBER(3)
SQL> alter table student add (m3 number(3), total number(3),
    result char(4));
Table altered.

SQL> desc student;
    Name                              Null?     Type
    -------------------------------   --------  ----
    RNO                                         NUMBER(5)
    SNAME                                       VARCHAR2(15)
    M1                                          NUMBER(3)
    M2                                          NUMBER(3)
    M3                                          NUMBER(3)
    TOTAL                                       NUMBER(3)
    RESULT                                      CHAR(4)
SQL> alter table student modify (result varchar2(4));
Table altered.

SQL> desc student;
    Name                              Null?     Type
    -------------------------------   --------  ----
    RNO                                         NUMBER(5)
    SNAME                                       VARCHAR2(15)
    M1                                          NUMBER(3)
```

```
    M2                                          NUMBER(3)
    M3                                          NUMBER(3)
    TOTAL                                       NUMBER(3)
    RESULT                                      VARCHAR2(4)
```

2.4.2.3 drop

This command drops (erase) the table from the database.

General format:

```
drop table <table-name>
```

Example:

```
SQL> desc student;
    Name                              Null?     Type
    -------------------------------   --------  ----
    RNO                                         NUMBER(5)
    SNAME                                       VARCHAR2(15)
    M1                                          NUMBER(3)
    M2                                          NUMBER(3)
    M3                                          NUMBER(3)
    TOTAL                                       NUMBER(3)
    RESULT                                      VARCHAR2(4)

SQL> drop table student;
Table dropped.
SQL> desc student;
Object does not exist.
```

2.4.3 Integrity Constraints

These constraints avoid invalid data entries into the table.

2.4.3.1 'not null' constraint

Generally, all the columns may have *'null'* values. When a *'not null'* constraint is used on a column, then that column will not allow *null* values.

Example:

```
SQL> create table stud (rno number(5) not null, sname varchar2(15));

Table created.

SQL> insert into stud (rno) values (1001);

1 row created.

SQL> insert into stud (sname) values ('IBRAHIM');
insert into stud (sname) values ('IBRAHIM')
```

```
         *
ERROR at line 1:
ORA-01400: cannot insert NULL into ("PG01"."STUD"."RNO")
```

The user must specify a value for *"rno"* in a row of the *stud* table; that column should not be *null*.

2.4.3.2 'primary key' Constraint

When it is set on a column, it avoids duplication value as well as *'null'* value to that column.

Example:

```
SQL> create table stud (rno number(5) Primary key, sname varchar2(15));

Table created.

SQL> insert into stud values (10001, 'Ibrahim');

1 row created.

SQL> insert into stud values (10002, null);

1 row created.

SQL> insert into stud values (null, 'Kannan');
     insert into stud values (null, 'Kannan')
         *
ERROR at line 1:
ORA-01400: cannot insert NULL into ("PG01"."STUD"."RNO")

SQL> insert into stud values (10001, 'Kannan');
     insert into stud values (10001, 'Kannan')
         *
ERROR at line 1:
ORA-00001: unique constraint (PG01.SYS_C002030) violated
```

The user must specify a *unique* value and not a *null value* or already used value to *rno* column in the table.

2.4.3.3 'check' constraint

The given value will be stored on the column if and only if the specified condition is true.

Example:

```
SQL> create table stud (rno number(5),
                      mark number(3) check (mark >= 0 and mark <= 100) );
Table created.

SQL> insert into stud values (1001, 60);
```

```
1 row created.

SQL> insert into stud values (1001, -60);
insert into stud values (1001, -60)
        *
ERROR at line 1:
ORA-02290: check constraint (PG01.SYS_C002031) violated

SQL> insert into stud values (1001, 160);
insert into stud values (1001, 160)
        *
ERROR at line 1:
ORA-02290: check constraint (PG01.SYS_C002031) violated
```

The given mark is stored in the mark column, if and only if the mark is within the range 0 and 100.

2.4.4 DDL Commands

The Data Definition Language (DDL) commands are used to manipulate data on tables.

2.4.4.1 insert

This command is used to insert one / more value(s) to column(s) of a table.

General format:

To insert values for all the columns of a table,

```
insert into <table-name> values (list of values)
```

To insert values for particular columns of a table,

```
insert into <table-name> (column-names) values (list of values)
```

If many (more than one value) are to be inserted, then the values should be separated by commas and the values for the data types *char, varchar2* and *date* should be enclosed within single quotes.

Example:

```
SQL> desc student;
    Name                              Null?     Type
    -------------------------------   --------  ---------
    RNO                                         NUMBER(5)
    SNAME                                       VARCHAR2(15)
    M1                                          NUMBER(3)
    M2                                          NUMBER(3)
    M3                                          NUMBER(3)
    TOTAL                                       NUMBER(3)
    RESULT                                      VARCHAR2(4)
SQL> insert into student (rno, sname, m1, m2, m3) values
                          (1001, 'IBRAHIM', 60, 70, 80);
```

```
1 row created.

SQL>  insert into student (rno, sname, m1, m2, m3) values
                               (&rno, '&sname', &m1, &m2, &m3);
Enter value for rno: 1002
Enter value for sname: KUMAR
Enter value for m1: 65
Enter value for m2: 86
Enter value for m3: 92
old   1:  insert into student (rno, sname, m1, m2, m3) values
                                   (&rno, '&sname', &m1, &m2, &m3)
new   1:  insert into student (rno, sname, m1, m2, m3) values
                                   (1002, 'KUMAR', 65, 86, 92)

1 row created.

SQL> insert into student (rno, sname, m1, m2, m3) values
                              (1003, 'RAHMAN', 49, 50, 55);
1 row created.
```

2.4.4.2 select

This command selects the required rows from the specified tables.

General format:

```
select column-name1, column-name2, ... from table1, table2, ...
where condition
```

The symbol '*' represents all the columns of a specified table.

Example:

```
SQL> select * from student;

     RNO  SNAME                 M1        M2        M3     TOTAL  RESU
--------  --------------   -------   -------   -------   -------  -----
    1001  IBRAHIM               60        70        80       210  PASS
    1002  KUMAR                 65        86        92       243  PASS
    1003  RAHMAN                49        50        55       154  FAIL

SQL> select rno, result from student;
     RNO
     RNO  RESU
--------  ----
    1001  PASS
    1002  PASS
    1003  FAIL
```

```
SQL> select * from student where rno=1002;
     RNO SNAME                   M1        M2        M3     TOTAL RESU
 ------- --------------- ------- ------- ------- ------- ----
    1002 KUMAR                   65        86        92       243 PASS

SQL> select * from student where result='PASS';
     RNO SNAME                   M1        M2        M3     TOTAL RESU
-------- --------------- ------- ------- ------- ------- ----
    1001 IBRAHIM                 60        70        80       210 PASS
    1002 KUMAR                   65        86        92       243 PASS
```

Selecting a range of records:

Create a table named "test" with two fields "id" and "name", and insert some records.

```
SQL> select * from test;
       ID NAME
--------- ----------
        1 one
        2 two
        3 three
        4 four
        5 five
        6 six
        7 seven
        8 eight
        9 nine
       10 ten
10 rows selected.
```

The following query retrieves first three records from "test" table. The keyword "rownum" refers the logical row number of the query result.

```
SQL> select * from test where rownum <= 3;
       ID NAME
--------- ----------
        1 One
        2 Two
        3 Three
```

The following query retrieves third records from "test" table.

```
SQL> select * from (select rownum rec, t.* from test t) where rec = 3;
     REC            ID NAME
--------   ---------- ----------
       3             3 Three
```

The following query retrieves a range of records from "test" table.

```
SQL> select * from (select rownum rec, t.* from test t)
where rec between 3 and 6;
```

```
     REC         ID  NAME
--------  ---------- ----------
       3          3  Three
       4          4  Four
       5          5  Five
       6          6  Six
```

2.4.4.3 *update*

This command is used to update (change) the existing values in a table.

General format:

```
update <table-name> set column-name=value1, column-name2=value2, ...
                                                     where condition
```

Example:

```
SQL> select * from student;
     RNO SNAME                 M1        M2        M3    TOTAL  RESU
----------------------  -------  -------  -------  --------  ----
    1001 IBRAHIM               60        70        80
    1002 KUMAR                 65        86        92
    1003 RAHMAN                49        50        55

SQL> update student set total=m1+m2+m3;

3 rows updated.

SQL> update student set result='PASS' where m1>=50 and m2>=50 and m3>=50;

2 rows updated.

SQL> update student set result='FAIL' where m1<50 or m2<50 or m3<50;

1 row updated.

SQL> select * from student;
     RNO SNAME                 M1        M2        M3    TOTAL  RESU
----------------------  -------  -------  -------  --------  ----
    1001 IBRAHIM               60        70        80      210  PASS
    1002 KUMAR                 65        86        92      243  PASS
    1003 RAHMAN                49        50        55      154  FAIL
```

2.4.4.4 *delete*

This command is used to delete the specified rows of a table.

General format:

```
delete from <table-name> where condition
```

Example:

```
SQL> select * from student;
      RNO  SNAME                         M1         M2         M3      TOTAL  RESU
-----------------------             -------    -------    -------   --------  ----
     1001  IBRAHIM                       60         70         80        210  PASS
     1002  KUMAR                         65         86         92        243  PASS
     1003  RAHMAN                        49         50         55        154  FAIL

SQL> delete from student where rno=1002;

1 row deleted.

SQL> select * from student;
      RNO  SNAME                         M1         M2         M3      TOTAL  RESU
--------   ---------------          -------    -------    -------   --------  ----
     1001  IBRAHIM                       60         70         80        210  PASS
     1003  RAHMAN                        49         50         55        154  FAIL

SQL> delete from student;
2 rows deleted.

SQL> select * from student;
no rows selected
```

2.4.5 Transaction Control Language (TCL)

All the changes (operations) made to the database in between a *commit* and/or a *rollback* operation is referred as a "*Transaction*".

2.4.5.1 commit

This command ends a transaction. The changes (made by transactions) are made permanent to the database.

General format:

```
commit
```

2.4.5.2 savepoint

A savepoint is a marker which represents a position in a transaction.

General format:

```
savepoint savepoint-id
```

2.4.5.3 rollback

This command is used to rollback (undo) the changes done in a table.

General format:

```
rollback to savepoint savepoint-id
```

Example:

```
SQL> create table stud (rno number(5), result varchar2(6));
Table created.

SQL> insert into stud values (1001, 'PASS');
1 row created.

SQL> insert into stud values (1002, 'FAIL');
1 row created.

SQL> insert into stud values (1003, 'PASS');
1 row created.

SQL> select * from stud;
     RNO  RESULT
--------  ------
    1001  PASS
    1002  FAIL
    1003  PASS

SQL> commit;
Commit complete.

SQL> select * from stud;
     RNO  RESULT
--------  ------
    1001  PASS
    1002  FAIL
    1003  PASS

SQL> update stud set result='PASS' where rno=1002;
1 row updated.

SQL> savepoint sp;
Savepoint created.

SQL> update stud set result='FAIL' where rno=1001;
1 row updated.

SQL> update stud set result='FAIL' where rno=1003;
1 row updated.
```

```
SQL> select * from stud;
     RNO  RESULT
--------  ------
    1001  FAIL
    1002  PASS
    1003  FAIL

SQL> rollback to savepoint sp;
Rollback complete.

SQL> select * from stud;
     RNO  RESULT
--------  ------
    1001  PASS
    1002  PASS
    1003  PASS

SQL> rollback;
Rollback complete.

SQL> select * from stud;
     RNO  RESULT
--------  ------
    1001  PASS
    1002  FAIL
    1003  PASS

SQL> update stud set result='PASS' where rno=1002;
1 row updated.

SQL> select * from stud;
     RNO  RESULT
--------  ------
    1001  PASS
    1002  PASS
    1003  PASS

SQL> commit;
Commit complete.

SQL> rollback;
Rollback complete.
```

```
SQL> select * from stud;
     RNO  RESULT
--------  ------
    1001  PASS
    1002  PASS
    1003  PASS
```

2.4.6 Referential Integrity (Functional Dependency)

It is a foreign key constraint, specifies a column/columns (these column/columns should be defined as primary key/unique key) of a table (named as referencing table or child table) as a foreign-key/foreign-keys on the referenced table (also named as parent-table).

When one table has a foreign key to another table, the referential integrity ensures that it is not allowed to add a record to the child table unless there is a corresponding record in the parent table. The cascading options (cascading update and cascading delete) ensure that changes made to the parent table are reflected in the child table. If the primary key for a record in the parent table changes, all corresponding records in the child table will be modified due to "cascading update" option, and if a record in the parent table is deleted, all corresponding records in the child table will be deleted due to "cascading delete" option.

General format

```
<child_table_column_definition> constraint <foreign_key_name> references
                        <parent_table_name>(<parent_table_column_names>)
                                                      [on delete cascade]
```

Example:

```
SQL> create table employee
     2 ( empnumber   number(5) primary key,
     3   empname     varchar2(20),
     4   salary      number(9,2)
     5 );
Table created.

SQL> create table address
     2 ( addressid    number(5) primary key,
     3   doornumber   varchar2(6) not null,
     4   streetname   varchar2(20),
     5   city         varchar2(20),
     6   country      varchar2(20),
     7   empnumber    number(5) references employee(empnumber) on
                      delete cascade
     8 );
Table created.
SQL> insert into employee (empnumber, empname, salary) values
     2               (1001, 'Mohamed Ibrahim', 98000.0);
1 row created.
```

```
SQL> insert into employee (empnumber, empname, salary) values
    2                 (1002, 'Kumar', 99000.0);
1 row created.

SQL> insert into address (addressid, doornumber, streetname, city, country,
    empnumber)
    2 values (2001, 'A-13-4', 'Jalan Bunus', 'Kuala Lumpur', 'Malaysia',
      1001);
1 row created.

SQL> insert into address (addressid, doornumber, streetname, city, country,
    empnumber)
    2 values (2002, 'B-15-2', 'Jalan TAR', 'Penang', 'Malaysia', 1002);
1 row created.

SQL> select * from employee;
     EMPNUMBER  EMPNAME                   SALARY
    ----------  --------------------  ----------
          1001  Mohamed Ibrahim            98000
          1002  Kumar                      99000

SQL> select * from address;
     ADDRESSID  DOORNU  STREETNAME     CITY          COUNTRY     EMPNUMBER
    ----------  ------  -------------  ------------  ---------   ---------
          2001  A-13-4  Jalan Bunus    Kuala Lumpur  Malaysia         1001
          2002  B-15-2  Jalan TAR      Penang        Malaysia         1002
```

Here, "employee" is the parent-table and "address" is the child-table. The column "empnumber" in the child-table refers the column "empnumber" of the parent-table on delete cascade. If we delete one record from "employee" table, then the corresponding child record in "address" table will also be deleted automatically.

```
SQL> delete from employee where empnumber=1001;
1 row deleted.

SQL> select * from employee;
     EMPNUMBER  EMPNAME                   SALARY
    ----------  --------------------  ----------
          1002  Kumar                      99000

SQL> select * from address;
     ADDRESSID  DOORNU  STREETNAME     CITY          COUNTRY     EMPNUMBER
    ----------  ------  -------------  ----------    ----------  ----------
          2002  B-15-2  Jalan TAR      Penang        Malaysia         1002
```

2.4.7 Set Operations

The set operations can be used to combine the results of two queries into a single one.

General format:

```
SelectStatement1 SetOperator SelectStatement2 where Condition
```

The allowed set operators are union, intersect and minus.

2.4.7.1 Union

This *union* operator returns all distinct rows selected by either query.

Example:

```
SQL> select * from stud1;
      RNO  RESULT
--------  ------
     1001  Pass
     1002  Fail
     1003  Pass

SQL> select * from stud2;
      RNO  RESULT
--------  ------
     1001  Pass
     1004  Fail

SQL> select * from stud1 union select * from stud2;
      RNO  RESULT
--------  ------
     1001  Pass
     1002  Fail
     1003  Pass
     1004  Fail
```

If you want all the rows from both tables use 'union all' instead of 'union'.

2.4.7.2 Intersect

This *intersect* operator returns only the rows that are retrieved by both queries.

Example:

```
SQL> select * from stud1 intersect select * from stud2;
      RNO  RESULT
--------  ------
     1001  Pass
```

2.4.7.3 Minus

This *minus* operator returns all distinct rows selected only by the first query and not by the second; the rows returned by the second query are matched with the rows returned by the first query, then such kind of rows are eliminated in the resultant rows.

Example:

```
SQL> select * from stud1 minus select * from stud2;
      RNO  RESULT
--------  ------
     1002  Fail
     1003  Pass
```

2.4.8 Join Operations

The join operations can be used to combine the data spread across the tables.

General format:

```
select column(s) from table(s) where join_condition
```

2.4.8.1 Simple Join

This retrieves the rows from two tables that are having a common column-name. Equi-join is based on equalities (only = symbol is used in condition). Non equi-join uses other relational operations such as <, <=, >, >=, <> in condition.

Example:

```
SQL> select * from st1;
      RNO  SNAME
--------  ---------------
     1000  Ibrahim
     1001  Kannan
     1003  Navas

SQL> select * from st2;
      RNO        TOTAL    RESULT
--------   ----------    ------
     1000          234    Pass
     1001          123    Fail
     1002          290    Pass

SQL> select * from st1, st2 where st1.rno=st2.rno;
      RNO  SNAME                    RNO      TOTAL   RESULT
--------  ---------------  --------  --------   ------
     1000  Ibrahim                  1000        234   Pass
     1001  Kannan                   1001        123   Fail
```

2.4.8.2 Self Join

It is used for joining of a table to itself, joins one row to another.

Example:

```
SQL> select s1.* from student s1, student s2
                                where s1.m1 > s2.m2 and s1.rno = s2.rno;
```

2.4.8.3 Outer Join

This will act as a simple join, and also retrieves rows from one table that do not match any row in other table. The symbol (+) represents outer joins.

Example:

```
SQL> select * from st1 , st2 where st1.rno(+) = st2.rno;
     RNO  SNAME                   RNO     TOTAL   RESULT
--------  ---------------  --------  --------   ------
    1000  Ibrahim                1000       234   Pass
    1001  Kannan                 1001       123   Fail
                                 1002       290   Pass
```

This query retrieves the rows which has the same *rno* value in both tables and also retrieves rows which are unique to *st2* (unmatched rows of *st2*). This process is also called as "Right Outer Join".

```
SQL> select * from st1, st2 where s1.rno = s2.rno(+);
     RNO  SNAME                   RNO     TOTAL   RESU
--------  ---------------- --------  --------   ------
    1000  Ibrahim                1000       234   Pass
    1001  Kannan                 1001       123   Fail
    1003  Navas
```

This query retrieves the rows which has the same *rno* value in both tables and also retrieves rows which are unique to *st1* (unmatched rows of *st1*). This join is also called as "Left Outer Join".

```
SQL> select * from st1 left outer join st2 on st1.rno = st2.rno;
     RNO  SNAME                   RNO     TOTAL   RESU
--------  ----------------  ------  -------   -------
    1000  Ibrahim                1000       234   Pass
    1001  Kannan                 1001       123   Fail
    1003  Navas
```

```
SQL> select * from st1 right outer join st2 on st1.rno = st2.rno;
     RNO  SNAME                   RNO     TOTAL   RESU
-------------------------   ------- ---------   ----
    1000  Ibrahim                1000       234   Pass
    1001  Kannan                 1001       123   Fail
                                 1002       290   Pass
```

2.4.9 Sub-queries

A query may contain another query for simplifying its operation, *i.e.*, nesting of such queries one within another is called sub-query. The sub-queries are written with in parenthesis.

Example:

```
SQL> select rno from st2 where total = (select max(total) from st2);
      RN
     RNO
 -------
    1002
```

2.4.10 Some Built-in Functions

The following are some of the built-in functions supported by Oracle.

2.4.10.1 Group Functions

`sum(x)`	Returns the summation of x in the group of records; The x is a column name.
`max(x)`	Returns the maximum of x in the group of records.
`min(x)`	Returns the minimum of x in the group of records.
`avg(x)`	Returns the average of x in the group of records.
`count(x)`	It returns the number of values present in the column x without including '*null*' values. The '*' may be given as argument to count all the rows of the table including duplicates and '*null*' values.

Examples:

```
SQL> select * from stud;
     RNO          MARK
--------    ----------
    1001            78
    1002            65
    1003            98
    1004            34
    1005            32

SQL> select sum(mark) from stud;
  SUM(MARK)
 ----------
        307

SQL> select max(mark) from stud;
  MAX(MARK)
 ----------
         98
```

```
SQL> select min(mark) from stud;
  MIN(MARK)
 ----------
         32

SQL> select avg(mark) from stud;
  AVG(MARK)
 ----------
       61.4

SQL> select count(*) from stud;
   COUNT(*)
 ----------
          5
```

2.4.10.2 Converting Functions

`To_char(date [,date-format])`	It converts *date* datatype value to *varchar2* datatype. The *'date-format'* specifies the format of the date in *varchar2* type. One can use the function `sysdate` for getting current date and time.
`To_date(char [,date-format]`	It converts *char* or *varchar2* datatype into *date* datatype. The *'date-format'* specifies the format of the date in *date* type. The `[,date-format]` section is optional.

Examples:

```
SQL> insert into emp (eno, doj) values (50001, '12-DEC-2005');
1 row created.

SQL>  insert into emp (eno, doj) values (50002, '07-JAN-2006');
1 row created.

SQL> insert into emp (eno, doj) values (50003,'11-FEB-2006');
1 row created.

SQL> select * from emp;
          ENO  DOJ
   ----------  ---------
        50001  12-DEC-05
        50002  07-JAN-06
        50003  11-FEB-06
```

```
SQL> select eno, to_char(doj,'dd/mm/yyyy') from emp;
         ENO  TO_CHAR(DO
  ----------  ----------
       50001  12/12/2005
       50002  07/01/2006
       50003  11/02/2006

SQL> insert into emp values (50004, to_date('01/01/2001','dd/mm/yyyy'));
1 row created.

SQL> select * from emp;
         ENO  DOJ
  ----------  ---------
       50001  12-DEC-05
       50002  07-JAN-06
       50003  11-FEB-06
       50004  01-JAN-01

SQL> insert into emp values (50005, sysdate);
1 row created.

SQL> select * from emp;
         ENO  DOJ
  ----------  ---------
       50001  12-DEC-05
       50002  07-JAN-06
       50003  11-FEB-06
       50004  01-JAN-01
       50005  22-JUN-07
5 rows selected.
```

2.4.11 View

A View may be considered as a logical table, which can be created using the following syntax.

```
create view <view_name> (view_column_names) as <select_query>
```

The table(s) upon which a view is based are called as *"base table(s)"*. The views can be accessed like normal tables; any change performed on a view will also be reflected on base table(s) and vice versa.

Example:

```
SQL> create table student
  2 ( rollnum   number(4) primary key,
  3   first_name varchar2(15),
  4   last_name  varchar2(15)
  5 );
```

```
Table created.

SQL> create table mark
     2 ( rollnum   number(4) primary key,
     3   mark1     number(3),
     4   mark2     number(3)
     5 );
Table created.

SQL> insert into student (rollnum, first_name, last_name)
     2 values (1001, 'Mohamed', 'Ibrahim');
1 row created.

SQL> insert into student (rollnum, first_name, last_name)
     2 values (1002, 'Karan', 'Singh');
1 row created.

SQL> insert into mark (rollnum, mark1, mark2) values (1001, 90, 80);
1 row created.

SQL> insert into mark (rollnum, mark1, mark2) values (1002, 10, 20);
1 row created.

SQL> create view student_view as
     2 select s.rollnum, s.first_name, m.mark1 from student s, mark m
     3 where s.rollnum = m.rollnum;
View created.

SQL> select * from student;
      ROLLNUM FIRST_NAME LAST_NAME
   ---------- ---------- ---------------
         1001 Mohamed    Ibrahim
         1002 Karan      Singh

SQL> select * from mark;
      ROLLNUM      MARK1      MARK2
   ---------- ---------- ----------
         1001         90         80
         1002         10         20
```

```
SQL> select * from student_view;
   ROLLNUM FIRST_NAME           MARK1
---------- --------------- ----------
      1001 Mohamed                 90
      1002 Karan                   10

SQL> delete from mark where rollnum = 1001;
1 row deleted.

SQL> select * from student_view;
   ROLLNUM FIRST_NAME           MARK1
 --------- --------------- ----------
      1002 Karan                   10

SQL> insert into student (rollnum, first_name, last_name)
     2 values (1003, 'Ravi', 'Chandren');
1 row created.

SQL> insert into mark (rollnum, mark1, mark2) values (1003, 50, 60);
1 row created.

SQL> select * from student_view;
   ROLLNUM FIRST_NAME           MARK1
---------- --------------- ----------
      1002 Karan                   10
      1003 Ravi                    50

SQL> update mark set mark1 = mark1 + 5, mark2 = mark2 + 4;
2 rows updated.

SQL> select * from mark;
   ROLLNUM           MARK1      MARK2
----------      ---------- ----------
      1002              15         24
      1003              55         64

SQL> select * from student_view;
   ROLLNUM FIRST_NAME           MARK1
---------- --------------- ----------
      1002 Karan                   15
      1003 Ravi                    55

SQL> update student_view set mark1 = mark1 + 10;
2 rows updated.
```

```
SQL> select * from student_view;
     ROLLNUM  FIRST_NAME                MARK1
  ----------  ---------------  ----------
        1002  Karan                        25
        1003  Ravi                         65

SQL> select * from mark;
     ROLLNUM              MARK1       MARK2
  ----------     ----------  ----------
        1002                 25          24
        1003                 65          64
```

2.4.12 Synonym

It creates synonym (alias name) to a database object (table, view, or sequence).

General format

```
create synonym <synonym_name> for <object_name>
```

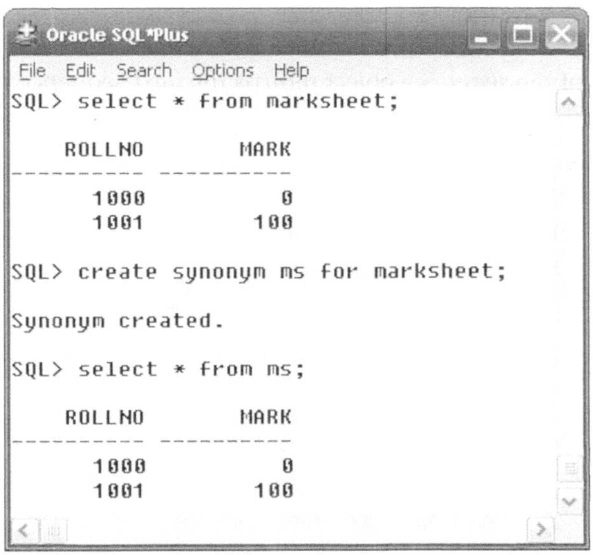

2.4.13 Sequence

It generates unique sequential integer numbers (generally used for Identity value of a table) in either ascending or descending order.

General format

```
create sequence <sequence-name>
     increment by n
     start with n
     [maxvalue n]
     [minvalue n]
     [cycle | nocycle]
```

where, 'n' refers an integer value and [] part is optional.

`increment by n`

Interval between two generated sequence numbers. If it is a positive value, then sequences are generated in ascending order; if it is a negative value, then the sequences are generated in descending order.

`start with n`

Specifies starting sequence number. It will be the next generated sequence number. It is not represent the minimum value in the sequence.

`maxvalue n`

Maximum sequence value in the sequence generation.

`minvalue n`

Minimum sequence value in the sequence generation.

`cycle`

Sequence numbers are generated in cyclic manner when maxvalue is reached in ascending order sequence generation or minvalue is reached in descending order sequence generation.

Example:

The nextval attribute of the sequence object returns the next sequence number.

```
SQL> create sequence marksheet_seq
     2 increment by 1
     3 minvalue 500
     4 maxvalue 1004
     5 start with 1001
     6 cycle;
Sequence created.

SQL> select marksheet_seq.nextval from dual;
        NEXTVAL
     ----------
           1001

SQL> select marksheet_seq.nextval from dual;
        NEXTVAL
     ----------
           1002

SQL> select * from marksheet;
         ROLLNO          MARK
     ----------    ----------
           1000             0
           1001           100
```

```
SQL> insert into marksheet (rollno, mark) values
2                          (marksheet_seq.nextval, 50);
1 row created.

SQL> select * from marksheet;
         ROLLNO            MARK
     ----------      ----------
           1003              50
           1000               0
           1001             100

SQL> select marksheet_seq.nextval from dual;
        NEXTVAL
     ----------
           1004

SQL> select marksheet_seq.nextval from dual;
        NEXTVAL
     ----------
            500

SQL> select marksheet_seq.nextval from dual;
        NEXTVAL
     ----------
            501
```

2.4.14 Dropping a Database Object

To drop (remove) a database object from the database, use the following command.

```
drop <database_object_type> <database_object_name>
```

where <database_object_type> refers a database object type such as table, view, synonym, and sequence.

Example:

```
SQL> desc student;
     Name             Null?          Type
     ------------     --------       --------------
     ROLLNUM          NOT NULL       NUMBER(4)
     FIRST_NAME                      VARCHAR2(15)
     LAST_NAME                       VARCHAR2(15)

SQL> drop table student;
Table dropped.

SQL> desc student;
```

```
ERROR:
ORA-04043: object student does not exist
```

2.4.15 Granting/Revoking Privileges

The privileges are rights to access database objects. It is mainly used to grant/revoke (set/reset) privileges to other users from one user. (There will be cases like; one project may require data which are maintained by another project. Instead of duplicating database table with values, we can give privileges to other project's users)

grant command:

Using this command, one user may give privilege to other user(s).

General format

```
grant <privileges> on <object_name> to <user_name>
```

One can also use the special word 'all' to represent all privileges that the object(s) have.

The "`with grant option`" (specified at the end of grant statement) makes the privileged user (the user, for whom the privileges are granted) to grant privileges on the privileging tables to other users.

revoke command:

This command withdraws (revokes) the privileges on an object, which has been granted to an user.

General format

```
revoke <privileges> on <object_name> from <user_name>
```

2.5 BACKUP AND RESTORE DATABASES

Oracle provides two utilities named 'exp' and 'imp' to export database to a dump file and import from a dump file respectively.

Simple formats of these utilities are given below:

Export specific table(s) to a dump file:

```
exp <local_oracle_user_name>/<password> file=<dump_file_name>
               tables=(<table_name1>, <table_name2>, ...)
imp <local_oracle_user_name>/<password> file=<dump_file_name> full=yes
```

2.6 PL/SQL

The PL/SQL (Procedural Language / Structured Query Language) is a procedural extension (supports decision making, looping, functions/procedures, etc.) of SQL. Usually, a PL/SQL block contains Data Manipulation Language (DML) and Transaction Control Language (TCL) statements.

The following are the three major parts of a PL/SQL block (program).

Declarative part

Executable statements part

Exception handling part

And the general format of a PL/SQL block looks below.

```
declare
      <declarative part>
begin
      <executable statements>
exception
      <exception handling statements>
end;
```

All the executable statements must be written within the begin and end key words. The objects/ variables, those are manipulated in this part must be declared in the declarative part. The runtime errors (*exceptions;* for example, dividing a number by zero) should be dealt in Exception handling part.

2.6.1 Operators

PL/SQL supports the following operators.

Arithmetic operators:

**	Exponentiation
*	Multiplication
/	Division
+	Addition
–	subtraction

Logical operators:

=	Equals to
!=	Not equals to
<	Less than
>	Greater than
<=	Less than or equals to
>=	Greater than or equals to

Assignment operator:

It is used to assign (set) some value to variables/constants.

The symbol for this operator is

:=

Concatenation operator:

This operator does catenation (combine two strings as single) on strings.

The symbol for this operator is

||

Range operator:

It represents range (from-to) values for numeric, character and date.

The symbol for this operator is

..

2.6.2 Comments

The symbol – is used for single line comments.

The symbol `/*      */` is used for multi-line comments.

Example:

```
-- This is single line comment

/* This
   is
   multi-line
   comment    */
```

2.6.3 Data Types

PL/SQL supports all the data types supported by SQL. The following are the additional data types those are supported by PL/SQL.

Boolean:

This data type is used to store either the values, TRUE, FALSE, or NULL. This is mainly used in conditional execution.

`Binary_integer`

This data type is used to represent singed integers (Size is 32 bit). One can also use its sub-data types.

`natural` (range is 0 to $2^{31}-1$)

`positive` (range is 1 to $2^{31}-1$)

Likewise, the programmers have the option to use the following sub-data types of number.

```
integer
real
```

2.6.4 Variable/Constant Declaration

All the variables/constants used in the PL/SQL block should be declared in the declarative part.

Variable declaration:

```
variable_name data_type;
```

The following syntax initializes the declared variable with the specified value at the declaration time.

```
variable_name data_type := initial_value;
```

You can also use the keyword '`default`' keyword instead of := symbol.

Constant declaration:

A constant represents fixed value which can not be altered during the execution of the program.

```
constant_name constant data_type := contant_value;
```

Here, '`constant`' is a keyword that tells the specified name is constant.

Like in variable declaration, you can use '`default`' keyword instead of := symbol.

Example:

Variables:

```
name1 varchar2(20);
name2 varchar2(20) := 'Ibrahim';
age1  integer;
age2  integer default 28;
```

Constants:

```
pi constant real := 3.1415;
pi constant real default 3.1415;
```

2.6.5 Attributes

PL/SQL variables/constants may have %type and %rowtype attributes, where %type represents a table's column, and %rowtype represents a row of a table.

Example:

```
declare
     empno  employee.eno%type;
     emprec employee%rowtype;
```

Then, the PL/SQL block variable empno has the same data type as the eno column of employee table is having. And emprec is now fit to hold an entire row of employee table. These types are very much used while manipulating cursors (which will be discussed later).

2.6.6 Control Structures

The following are the conditional constructs available in PL/SQL.

2.6.6.1 If Statement

General Format – I

```
if <condition> then
     statements
end if;
```

If the specified condition is true, then the specified *statements* will be executed.

General Format – II

```
if <condition> then
     statements_block1;
else
     statements_block2;
end if;
```

If the condition is true, then statements_block1 will be executed, otherwise (if the condition becomes false), then statements_block2 will be executed.

General Format – III

```
if <condition> then
     statements_block1;
```

```
elsif <condition> then
      statements_block2;
...
...
else
      statements_else_block;
end if;
```

When one of the specified conditions becomes true, then the corresponding `statements_block` will be executed. If none of the conditions is true, then the statements specified after `else` key word (`statements_else_block`) will be executed.

2.6.6.2 Case Statement

General Format

```
case <selector>
      when expression1 then statments1;
      when expression2 then statement2;
      ...
      ...
      else statements_else;
end case
```

If there is a match with the value of *expression* and the value of *selector*, then the corresponding *statements* will be executed. If there is no match, then the *statements* specified in *else* part will be executed.

```
case
      when booleanexpression1 then statments1;
      when booleanexpression2 then statments2;
      ...
      when booleanexpressionn then statmentsn;
      [ else statements_else; ]
end case
```

When one of the specified Boolean expressions became "true", then the corresponding statement bock will be executed, otherwise else part will be executed.

2.6.7 Looping Statements

The following are the iterative statements supported by PL/SQL.

2.6.7.1 loop .. end loop

General Format

```
loop
      <sequence of statements>
      exit when <condition>;
end loop;
```

If the condition specified in exit when statement becomes 'true', then the loop will end. If we are not using exit when statement in the above syntax, then the loop becomes infinite.

2.6.7.2 *while*

As long as the condition becomes true, the loop will be executed.

General Format

```
while <condition>
loop
      <sequence_of_statements>
end loop;
```

2.6.7.3 *for*

General Format I

```
for index in [reverse] lowerbound .. upperbound
loop
      <sequence_of_statements>
end loop;
```

Generally, the iteration proceeds from lower-bound to upper-bound. The '*reverse*' option makes the iteration to proceed from upper-bound to lower-bound.

General Format II

```
for <row_variable> in <list_of_values>
loop
      <sequence_of_statements>
end loop;
```

This format of for loop can be used with cursors (will be discussed later); it opens the cursor, iterates the loop by fetching each row from the cursor and assigns it on the row_variable, and closes the cursor.

2.6.7.4 *goto statement*

General Format

```
goto label
```

It is an unconditional jump statement, used to transfer control to a labelled location. A label should be closed by double angle brackets (<< `label`>>).

2.6.8 Exception Handling

An exception is an error at runtime (such as dividing a number by zero). When an exception us raised in a PL/SQL block, the control will be immediately transferred to the exception handling part. Then, the corresponding exception handling part will be executed. If no exception types matches, then system will give default error messages.

The syntax of exception handling part in PL/SQL part is given below.

```
exception
      when <exception_name> then
      exception_handling_statements;
```

```
...
...
when others then
exception_handling_statements;
```

The following are some of the pre-defined exceptions which will be raised automatically by the database if corresponding exceptions occurred. (Some of the keywords such as cursor are new to you; will be discussed later)

`cursor_already_open`

Raised when the program tries to open a cursor which is already opened

`invalid_cursor`

Raised when the program make invalid operation on cursor (For example, when cursor is not opened, the programmer tries to fetch data, or close the cursor).

`no_data_found`

Raised when the select statement retrieves no rows.

`too_many_rows`

Raised when the 'select into' statement (selecting database value(s) and putting into PL/SQL variable(s)) retrieves more than one row.

`dup_val_on_index`

Raised when the program tries to insert duplicate value for a column for which a *unique* key constraint was set.

`zero_error`

Raised when the program tries to divide a number by zero (divide by zero error).

`others`

This is a special keyword, which can be used to handle unspecified exceptions in the exception handling part.

User-defined Exceptions:

The user-defined exceptions must be declared in the declarative part of PL/SQL and should be invoked (raise) using raise statement explicitly.

Declaring:

```
<exception_name> exception
```

Invoking:

```
raise <exception_name>
```

2.6.9 Cursors

Oracle uses a work area to store the processing information. One can access this work area using 'cursor'. (For easy understanding, think a cursor as a logical table)

There are two types of cursors:

- Explicit cursor
- Implicit cursor.

Every cursor should be declared in the declarative part of PL/SQL using the syntax,

```
cursor <cursor_name> is <select_statement>
```

2.6.9.1 *Explicit Cursor*

A cursor must be opened before it is used in PL/SQL block.

```
open <cursor_name>
```

When a cursor is opened, the pointer points the first row in the cursor (if the select statement in cursor declaration retrieves row/rows). The rows in the cursor can be retrieved and stored in PL/SQL variables using fetch statement.

```
fetch <cursor_name> into <PL/SQL variable(s)>
```

The fetch statement fetches the current row (the row that the pointer is currently pointing) and puts it on the specified PL/SQL variables(s) and moves the pointer to the next row (if exists).

A cursor can be closed using close statement.

```
close <cursor_name>
```

Explicit cursor attributes:

These cursor attributes are used to get additional information about the cursor (data). Some important attributes are described below.

`%isopen`

It is true, if the cursor is currently opened, otherwise false.

`%found`

If the last fetch statement retrieves a row, then it becomes true; otherwise it becomes false.

`%notfound`

It is opposite to %found. If the last fetch statement does not retrieve any row, it becomes true; otherwise it becomes false.

`%rowcount`

This attributes gives the count of ***fetched*** rows from a cursor, it does not represent the total number of rows in a cursor. It gives the count that many number of rows retrieved from the associated cursor.

2.6.9.2 *Implicit Cursor*

It is also called as '`SQL cursor`' which refers the most recently executed SQL DML statement; however we can not fetch individual rows of resultant using this implicit cursor.

Oracle automatically opens and closes implicit cursor before and after the execution of its associated SQL statements. Always the implicit cursor name is '`sql`'.

These implicit cursors support the following attributes.

`%found`

If the associated SQL DML statement affects (including select) the rows in associated tables, it becomes true; otherwise it becomes false.

`%notfound`

If the SQL DML statement does not affect (including select) any rows in the table, it becomes true; otherwise it becomes false.

`%rowcount`

It gives the count of all rows which are affected (including select) by SQL DML statement.

Example:

The following PL/SQL calculates and updates required student data.

```
SQL> create table student
  2  ( rollnum   number(5),
  3    name      varchar2(15),
  4    mark1     number(3),
  5    mark2     number(3),
  6    mark3     number(3),
  7    total     number(3),
  8    average   number(5,2),
  9    result    varchar2(4),
 10    class     varchar2(15) );
Table created.

SQL> insert into student (rollnum, name, mark1, mark2, mark3) values
2    (1001, 'Ibrahim', 90, 93, 98);

SQL> insert into student (rollnum, name, mark1, mark2, mark3) values
2    (1002, 'Kumar', 60, 65, 64);
1 row created.

SQL> insert into student (rollnum, name, mark1, mark2, mark3) values
2    (1003, 'Ajay', 49, 80, 78);
1 row created.

SQL> insert into student (rollnum, name, mark1, mark2, mark3) values
2    (1004, 'Nitin', 52, 55, 54);
1 row created.

SQL> select * from student;
   ROLLNUM  NAME     MARK1   MARK2   MARK3   TOTAL   AVERAGE  RESU  CLASS
   -------  ------  -----  ------  ------ -------- --------  ----  -------
      1001  Ibrahim    90      93      98
      1002  Kumar      60      65      64
      1003  Ajay       49      80      78
      1004  Nitin      52      55      54
```

Store the following PL/SQL code in *marklist.sql* file (in our case, stored at C:)

```
declare
     rnum       student.rollnum%type;
     m1         student.mark1%type;
     m2         student.mark2%type;
     m3         student.mark3%type;
     m1total    number := 0;
```

```
        mlaverage number := 0;
        mlresult  varchar2(4);
        mlclass   varchar2(15) := ' --- ';
        cursor c is select rollnum, mark1, mark2, mark3 from student;

    begin
        open c;
        if c%isopen then
          loop
            fetch c into rnum, m1, m2, m3;
            exit when c%notfound;

            mltotal := m1 + m2 + m3;
            mlaverage := mltotal / 3;
          if m1 >= 50  and  m2 >= 50  and  m3 >= 50 then
            mlresult := 'PASS';
          else
            mlresult := 'FAIL';
          end if;

          if mlresult = 'PASS' then
            case
              when mlaverage >= 85 then mlclass := 'DISTINCTION';
              when mlaverage >= 60 then mlclass := 'FIRST';
              else mlclass := 'SECOND';
            end case;
          else
            mlclass := ' --- ';
          end if;

          update student set total = mltotal, average = mlaverage,
                        result = mlresult, class = mlclass
                        where rollnum = rnum;
        end loop;
        close c;
        commit;
        dbms_output.put_line('Process completed.');
    else
        dbms_output.put_line('The cursor is not opened.');
        end if;
    end;
/
```

Then, Invoke this file at SQL prompt as follows.

```
Oracle SQL*Plus
File Edit Search Options Help
SQL> select * from student;

   ROLLNUM NAME                 MARK1      MARK2      MARK3      TOTAL    AVERAGE RESU CLASS
---------- --------------- ---------- ---------- ---------- ---------- ---------- ---- ---------------
      1001 Ibrahim                 90         93         98
      1002 Kumar                   60         65         64
      1003 Ajay                    49         80         78
      1004 Nitin                   52         55         54
```

```
Oracle SQL*Plus
File Edit Search Options Help
SQL> @C:\marklist.sql
Process completed.

PL/SQL procedure successfully completed.

SQL> select * from student;

   ROLLNUM NAME                 MARK1      MARK2      MARK3      TOTAL    AVERAGE RESU CLASS
---------- --------------- ---------- ---------- ---------- ---------- ---------- ---- ---------------
      1001 Ibrahim                 90         93         98        281      93.67 PASS DISTINCTION
      1002 Kumar                   60         65         64        189         63 PASS FIRST
      1003 Ajay                    49         80         78        207         69 FAIL ---
      1004 Nitin                   52         55         54        161      53.67 PASS SECOND
```

The above code selects individual columns and assigns to PL/SQL variables for manipulation. The above code can be written as follows, which fetches entire row for manipulation.

```
declare
     cursor c is select * from student;
     r c%rowtype;
     begin
     open c;
     if c%isopen then
       loop
         fetch c into r;
         exit when c%notfound;

         r.total := r.mark1 + r.mark2 + r.mark3;
         r.average := r.total / 3;

         if r.mark1 >= 50  and  r.mark2 >= 50  and  r.mark3 >= 50 then
             r.result := 'PASS';
         else
             r.result := 'FAIL';
         end if;

         if r.result = 'PASS' then
            case
              when r.average >= 85 then r.class := 'DISTINCTION';
```

```
            when r.average >= 60 then r.class := 'FIRST';
            else r.class := 'SECOND';
          end case;
        else
          r.class := ' --- ';
        end if;

        update student set total = r.total, average = r.average,
                    result = r.result, class = r.class
                    where rollnum = r.rollnum;
        end loop;
        close c;
        commit;
        dbms_output.put_line('Process completed.');
      else
        dbms_output.put_line('The cursor is not opened.');
      end if;
    end;
/
```

The above code can also be written using a specialised for loop as below.

```
declare
    cursor c is select * from student;
    r c%rowtype;

    begin
      for r in c
      loop
        r.total := r.mark1 + r.mark2 + r.mark3;
        r.average := r.total / 3;

        if r.mark1 >= 50  and  r.mark2 >= 50  and  r.mark3 >= 50 then
          r.result := 'PASS';
        else
          r.result := 'FAIL';
        end if;

        if r.result = 'PASS' then
          case
            when r.average >= 85 then r.class := 'DISTINCTION';
            when r.average >= 60 then r.class := 'FIRST';
            else r.class := 'SECOND';
          end case;
        else
```

```
            r.class := ' --- ';
        end if;

        update student set total = r.total, average = r.average,
                    result = r.result, class = r.class
                    where rollnum = r.rollnum;
        end loop;
        dbms_output.put_line('Process completed.');
      end;
  /
```

Exception handling example:

The following program uses exception handling mechanism to check whether all the records in the student table have the result status 'PASS'. Store the content in *C:\marklist.sql* file.

Note: We can achieve the above goal using a single SQL statement; however the exception handling is applied for illustration purpose.

```
    declare
        exception_fail exception;

        cursor c is select * from student;
        r c%rowtype;

        begin
        for r in c
        loop
          dbms_output.put_line('Verifying record');
          if r.result = 'PASS' then
            dbms_output.put_line(r.rollnum || '   PASS');
          else
            raise exception_fail;
          end if;
            dbms_output.put_line('Verified');
          end loop;

          dbms_output.put_line('All students have ''PASS'' result.');

          exception
            when exception_fail then
              dbms_output.put_line('This Table contains Failed student data.');
          dbms_output.put_line('Process completed.');
        end;
    /
```

```
Oracle SQL*Plus
File Edit Search Options Help
SQL> select * from student;

  ROLLNUM NAME                 MARK1      MARK2      MARK3      TOTAL    AVERAGE RESU CLASS
---------- --------------- ---------- ---------- ---------- ---------- ---------- ---- ---------------
      1001 Ibrahim                90         93         98        281      93.67 PASS DISTINCTION
      1002 Kumar                  60         65         64        189         63 PASS FIRST
      1003 Ajay                   49         80         78        207         69 FAIL ---
      1004 Nitin                  52         55         54        161      53.67 PASS SECOND

SQL> @C:\marklist.sql
Verifying record
1001    PASS
Verified
Verifying record
1002    PASS
Verified
Verifying record
This Table contains Failed student data.
Process completed.

PL/SQL procedure successfully completed.
```

2.6.10 Triggers

A database trigger is a stored program that will be fired (executed, triggered) whenever the associated table is accessed to insert, update, or delete values. These triggers are mainly used to validate the data before storing into database.

A trigger can be created/replaced using the following syntax.

```
create or replace trigger <trigger-name>
[before|after] [insert|delete|update] on
<table_name> [for each row]
<declaration>
begin
      <statements>
end;
```

Here, square brackets `[]` represents optional part, and pipe symbol '|' represents options (choosing options).

Once the trigger was created, whenever the associated table is referred using DML statements (insert, delete, update), the trigger will be fired. These DMS statements, which will made to fire a trigger, are called "Triggering Statements". If '`before`' option is used, then the trigger will be fired before doing the operation (before executing the triggering statements). Likewise, if '`after`' option is used, then the trigger will be executed after triggering statements were executed. The '`for each row`' option will make the trigger to fire once per (affecting) row in the corresponding table.

To display user-defined error messages, Oracle provides a function which has the following syntax,

```
raise_application_error(error_number,'error_message')
```

The `error_number` should be within the range -20000 to -20999.

An active trigger can be disabled by using the following command.

```
alter trigger <trigger_name> disable
```

In the following example, I am writing a Trigger which will validate 'mark' entry into 'marksheet' table.

I am setting the allowed range for mark is 0–100. When somebody tries to insert/update invalid mark (out of the range 0–100), then the trigger will be fired and invalid entry will not be done with the table.

```
Oracle SQL*Plus
File Edit Search Options Help

SQL> insert into marksheet (rollno, mark) values (1000, 0);

1 row created.

SQL> insert into marksheet (rollno, mark) values (1001, 100);

1 row created.

SQL> select * from marksheet;

    ROLLNO       MARK
---------- ----------
      1000          0
      1001        100
```

```
Oracle SQL*Plus
File Edit Search Options Help
SQL> create table marksheet (
  2  rollno number(5) primary key,
  3  mark   number(3)
  4  );

Table created.

SQL> set serveroutput on;
SQL> create or replace trigger mark_trigger
  2      before insert or update on marksheet for each row
  3  begin
  4      if (:new.mark < 0   or    :new.mark > 100) then
  5       raise_application_error(-20000, 'Invalid mark. Mark should be with in the range 0 - 100');

  6      end if;
  7  end;
  8  /

Trigger created.
```

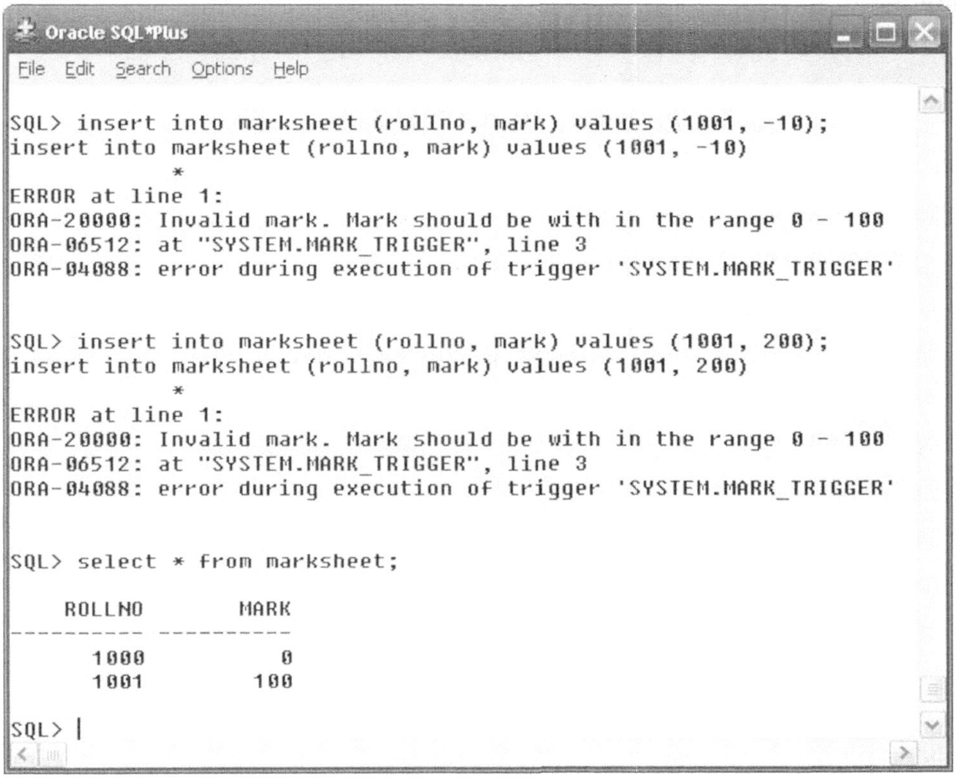

```
SQL> insert into marksheet (rollno, mark) values (1001, -10);
insert into marksheet (rollno, mark) values (1001, -10)
            *
ERROR at line 1:
ORA-20000: Invalid mark. Mark should be with in the range 0 - 100
ORA-06512: at "SYSTEM.MARK_TRIGGER", line 3
ORA-04088: error during execution of trigger 'SYSTEM.MARK_TRIGGER'


SQL> insert into marksheet (rollno, mark) values (1001, 200);
insert into marksheet (rollno, mark) values (1001, 200)
            *
ERROR at line 1:
ORA-20000: Invalid mark. Mark should be with in the range 0 - 100
ORA-06512: at "SYSTEM.MARK_TRIGGER", line 3
ORA-04088: error during execution of trigger 'SYSTEM.MARK_TRIGGER'


SQL> select * from marksheet;

    ROLLNO       MARK
---------- ----------
      1000          0
      1001        100

SQL> |
```

2.6.11 Stored Procedures

Generally, these procedures are used to perform the actions which are required frequently. Even though, stored procedures are precompiled and executed fast, one disadvantage will arise when you pass more parameters to stored procedures while calling from Java code.

General format for creating a stored procedure:

```
create procedure <procedure-name> (<parameter-list>) is
     <local_variable_declarations>;
begin
     Procedure_body
end;
```

There are three types of modes for passing arguments.

- Passing **value(s)** and do not return value from procedure (in mode)
- Passing **no value** (of course, you should pass variable name to get value), but returning **value** (out mode)
- Passing initial **value** and returning the updated **value** (in out mode).

If the user does not specify any mode, then the 'in' mode is taken by default.

Examples:

(*i*) **in Parameter**

```
Oracle SQL*Plus
File Edit Search Options Help
SQL> select * from st1;

       RNO SNAME
---------- --------------------
      1000 Ibrahim
      1003 Navas
      1001 Kannan

SQL> create procedure del (rollno in number) is
  2  begin
  3    delete from st1 where st1.rno = rollno;
  4  end;
  5  /

Procedure created.

SQL> begin
  2    del(1003);
  3  end;
  4  /

PL/SQL procedure successfully completed.

SQL> select * from st1;

       RNO SNAME
---------- --------------------
      1000 Ibrahim
      1001 Kannan

SQL> |
```

(*ii*) **out Parameter**

```
Oracle SQL*Plus
File Edit Search Options Help
SQL> create or replace procedure tempconversion (f in number, c out number) is
  2  begin
  3   c := 5.0/9.0 * (f-32.0);
  4  end;
  5  /

Procedure created.

SQL> set serveroutput on;
SQL>
SQL> declare
  2   tempf number(5,2);
  3   tempc number(5,2);
  4
  5  begin
  6   tempf := &tempf;
  7   tempconversion(tempf, tempc);
  8   dbms_output.put_line('Temperature: ' || to_char(tempf) ||
  9                       'F = ' || to_char(tempc) || 'C');
 10  end;
 11  /
Enter value for tempf: 98.4
old   6:  tempf := &tempf;
new   6:  tempf := 98.4;
Temperature: 98.4F = 36.89C

PL/SQL procedure successfully completed.

SQL>
```

(*iii*) **in out Parameter**

```
Oracle SQL*Plus
File Edit Search Options Help
SQL> create or replace procedure netpay (salary in out number) is
  2  deductions number;
  3  begin
  4   deductions := salary * 0.15;
  5   salary:=salary - deductions;
  6  end;
  7  /

Procedure created.

SQL> set serveroutput on;
SQL>
SQL> declare
  2   pay number(8,2);
  3  begin
  4   pay := &pay;
  5   dbms_output.put_line('The Grosspay is ' || to_char(pay));
  6   netpay(pay);
  7   dbms_output.put_line('The Netpay is ' || to_char(pay));
  8  end;
  9  /
Enter value for pay: 78000.00
old   4:  pay := &pay;
new   4:  pay := 78000.00;
The Grosspay is 78000
The Netpay is 66300

PL/SQL procedure successfully completed.

SQL> |
```

2.6.12 Functions

A function is a name given to a group of statements like procedures, but always returns one value.

General format

```
create or replace function <function_name>(arguments)
                                return <datatype> is
<local_variable_declarations>
begin
     Function_body
end;
```

Example:

The following is a recursive function, which returns the factorial of a specified number as argument.

Store the following function code in *C:\financial.sql* file.

```
create or replace function factorial(n number) return number is f number;
begin
     if n = 0  or n = 1 then
       return 1;
     else
       f := n * factorial(n-1);
     end if;
     return f;
end;
/
```

Create the function as shown below.

```
SQL> @C:\factorial.sql
Function created.
```

Invoke the function as shown below. You can call this function in PL/SQL blocks also, as like built-in functions.

```
SQL> select factorial(4) from dual;
 FACTORIAL(4)
 ------------
           24
```

SUMMARY

In this chapter, the Oracle installation procedure for both MS Windows platform is given. The DDL, DML, and TCL commands are explained with suitable examples. The database objects such as synonyms, and sequences are explained with their general formats. The PL/SQL for Oracle is explained in detail with sample code. The stored procedures are neatly explained, which can be called by an application through database connectivity to minimise database interactions in performing bulk database operations.

Chapter 3

WORKING WITH MySQL DATABASE

3.0 INTRODUCTION

MySQL is one of the popular Relational Database Management System (RDBMS), open source software under the GNU Public License (GPL). It was originally developed and released by MySQL AB, and it is now owned, further developed and supported by Sun Microsystems. This chapter illustrates how to work with MySQL.

3.1 INSTALLING MySQL

The "MySQL" software is a product from Sun Microsystems, can be downloaded from MySQL's official website, http://www.mysql.com. Download the latest Generally Available (GA) version of MySQL, in our case; I am downloading MySQL 5.1. Click on "Downloads" links and click "Download" button of MySQL Community Server. Then, click the link MySQL Community Server 5.1 on the left panel. Choose required download (for your platform, MS Windows, Linux ...). I am downloading "mysql-5.1.32-win32.msi" (Windows MSI Installer for x86). Write script to download for Linux. Also, download MySQL GUI Tools, which provides Graphical User Interface for working with MySQL. In our case, I am downloading "mysql-gui-tools-5.0-r17-win32.msi" (GUI Tool for Windows).

3.1.1 Installation Procedure for MS Windows

Double click on "mysql-5.1.32-win32.msi" file. Let the Setup Type be "Typical". While continuing this installation procedure, "Configure the MySQL Server now" checkbox will be checked by default, accept the default to configure MySQL. Choose "Standard Configuration" radio button (assumed that MySQL is not currently installed in your compute) and proceed. Enter root (MySQL Administrator) password and confirm the same. Then, press "Execute" button. You can change the configuration details (reconfiguration) by invoking "MySQL Server Instance Config Wizard" from Windows Start → Programs → MySQL menu.

Double click on "mysql-gui-tools-5.0-r17-win32.msi" to install GUI interface for MySQL and following the default settings. However, this version of the tool is not suitable for MySQL 6. Download and install latest version of this GUI tool when it became available.

Testing MySQL Installation:

Start MySQL service (Invoke Service window through Control Panel, and start required MySQL service).

Open command window (DOS Window / Shell Window) and issue the following command.

```
mysql –u root –p<root_password>
```

Note that you are logging as system administrator (root) with his password (if specified earlier). Note that there is no space between –p and `<root_password>`.

```
C:\Users\Ibrahim> mysql -u root -pibrahim
Welcome to the MySQL monitor.  Commands end with ; or \g.
Your MySQL connection id is 32
Server version: 6.0.10-alpha-community MySQL Community Server (GPL)

Type 'help;' or '\h' for help. Type '\c' to clear the buffer.

mysql>
```

3.2 CREATING/DROPPING A DATABASE SCHEMA

A schema (defines tables and views in a database together with the relationships) can be created using the following command.

Open DOS window, and login to MySQL as root. Then, use the following command to create a database named "*demodb*".

```
mysql> create database demodb;
Query OK, 1 row affected (0.00 sec)
```

If you want to drop an existing database, use the following command.

```
drop database <database-name>
```

We can use MySQL Query Browser GUI tool also to create schema as described below.

Open MySQL Query Browser (Start → Programs → MySQL → MySQL Query browser) and login as 'root'.

Right click on the "Schemata" tab and select "Create New Schema" and specify the schema-name.

To drop a schema, select it and right click, then choose "Drop Schema".

3.3 CREATING/DROPPING A USER

We can add/delete users using GUI tool or using SQL commands.

Using GUI interface:

To create a user, invoke the "MySQL Administrator" window from Windows Start menu (Start → Programs → MySQL → MySQL Administration) and login as 'root'. Choose "User Administration" on the left panel, and then click on "Add new user" button on the right of that panel. Specify MySQL User Name and Password in "User Information" tab, and assign privileges for the available schemas in "Schema Privileges" tab, and additional configurations in "Resources" tab. Finally click on "Apply changes" button to commit.

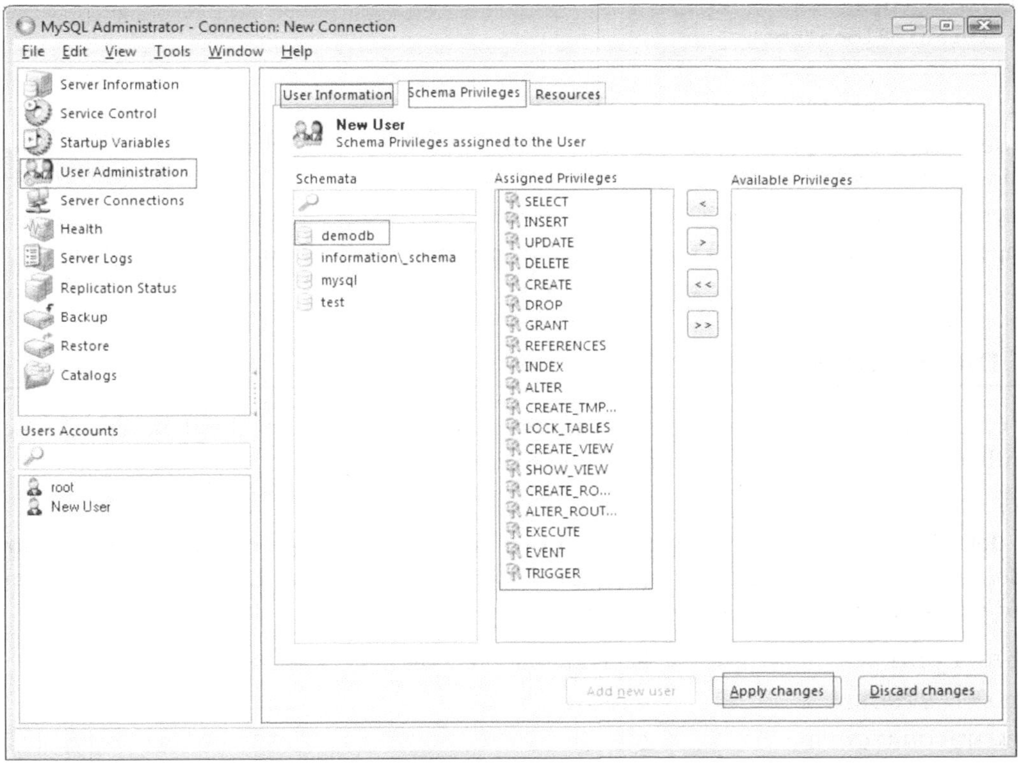

Fig. 3.1 Creating a user using MySQL GUI Tool

To drop a user, choose the user in "User Administrator" screen on MySQL Administrator window. Right click and choose "Delete user".

Using SQL commands:

The following command creates a user named *"ibrahim"* with password *"pword"* and sets necessary rights for *ibrahim* on the database *demodb*.

```
mysql> grant all privileges on demodb.* to ibrahin@localhost
    ->        identified by 'pword' with grant option;
Query OK, 0 rows affected (0.00 sec)
```

Now, try to login as *ibrahim* for the database *demodb*.

```
C:\Users\Ibrahim> mysql -u ibrahim -ppword demodb
Welcome to the MySQL monitor.  Commands end with ; or \g.
Your MySQL connection id is 33
Server version: 6.0.10-alpha-community MySQL Community Server (GPL)

Type 'help;' or '\h' for help. Type '\c' to clear the buffer.

mysql> select user();
+--------------------+
| user()             |
+--------------------+
| ibrahim@localhost  |
+--------------------+
1 row in set (0.02 sec)
```

To delete a user, login as 'root' and revoke the assigned privileges on the user and delete the user using 'delete user' command.

```
mysql> show grants for ibrahim@localhost;
mysql> revoke all privileges, grant option from ibrahim@localhost;
mysql> drop user ibrahim@localhost;
```

3.4 DATA TYPES

A data type should be specified for each column of the table. Some of the data types, which are frequently used in MySQL database tables, are given below:

Numeric types:

By default, all data types are signed, so that we can store negative and positive numbers. The reserved word "SIGNED" may be used to explicitly specify that the data type is singed. The reserved word "UNSIGNED" is used to specify unsigned version of a data type.

Data Type	Minimum Value	Maximum Value
TINYINT SINGED	-128	127
TINYINT UNSIGNED	0	255
SMALLINT SIGNED	-32768	32767
SMALLINT UNSIGNED	0	65535
MEDIUMINT SINGED	-8388608	8388607
MEDIUMINT UNSIGNED	0	16777215
INT SIGNED, INTEGER SINGED	-2147483648	2147483647
INT UNSIGNED, INTEGER UNSIGNED	0	4294967295
BIGINT SINGED	-9223372036854775808	9223372036854775807
BIGINT UNSIGNED	0	18446744073709551615

`BIT`	`0 or 1`
`BOOL, BOOLEAN`	`true or false`
`FLOAT, FLOAT(M, D)`	`M digits in total (excluding dot and minus sign, if present), in which D digits may be after decimal part. MySQL does rounding of the result while shirking to specified precision`

`DOUBLE,`
`DOUBLE PRECISION(M, D),`
`REAL(M, D)`
	`Double precision length data`

`NUMERIC, DECIMAL,` `DECIMAL(M,D), DEC(M, D)`	`Use to store both integer and floating point numbers. Specify D as 0 to represent whole numbers`

String types:

Date Type	Range
`CHAR`	0 to 255 Characters
`VARCHAR`	0 to 65535 Characters If the user enters a value that is shorter than the specified length, then the database would blank-pad to the fixed length in *char* data type so that memory will be allocated for the column's length, but in *varchar* data type, the column's length is assumed as the user entered datum's length plus datum identifying the length of data (usually, 1 or 2 bytes).

Date types:

Date Type	Range
`DATETIME`	`YYYY-MM-DD HH:MM:SS`
`TIMESTAMP`	`YYYY-MM-DD HH:MM:SS` The value of this data type is displayed as DATETIME data type. The difference: TIMESTAMP values are converted to UTC (Coordinated Universal Time) time from current system time zone before storage and converted back to current system time zone from UTC for retrieval.
`DATE`	`YYYY-MM-DD`
`TIME`	`HH:MM:SS`
`YEAR`	`YYYY`

Storing binary and large data:

M – Size specified for the column

L – Actual length of datum, will be stored on that column

Date Type	Range
BINARY(M)	M bytes; Range 0 - 255
VARBINARY(M)	If L <= 255, then size is L + 1 bytes; If L > 255, then size is L + 2 bytes
TINYBLOB, TINYTEXT	L + 1 bytes, where L < 2^{8}
BLOB, TEXT	L + 2 bytes, where L < 2^{16}
MEDIUMBLOB, MEDIUMTEXT	L + 3 bytes, where L < 2^{24}
LONGBLOB, LONGTEXT	L + 4 bytes, where L < 2^{32}

ENUM type:

An ENUM type column can store a value from already enumerated list of values.

```
ENUM('value1', 'value2', ...)
```

SET type:

An SET type column can store zero, one, or more values from already specified list of values.

```
SET('value1', 'value2', ...)
```

3.5 SQL COMMANDS

We can use GUI based SQL client to easily work with MySQL. However, command based interface will be required for development of applications (using JDBC, ADO), which interact with database. And it is very handy when accessing database from remote systems. Some of the basic SQL statements are explained below.

Data definition commands:

```
create database <database_name>
```

Creates a database schema.

To change to a database schema, use "use <database_name>"

```
create table <table_name> (columns_specification)

column_specification includes,

column_name data_type
column_name data_type CONSTRAINT key_name PRIMARY KEY
column_name data_type CONSTRAINT key_name UNIQUE
column_name data_type PRIMARY KEY AUTO_INCREMENT
```

Creates a table in the current (use) schema. Use the following statemnt to create a new table from an existing table. Note that the records will not be copied from existing table to new table.

```
create table <new_table_name> like <existing_table_name>
```

The following statement creates a table from an existing table with records.

```
create table <new_table_name> as
                select <columns> from <existing_table>
```

```
create view <view_name> [(column_names)] as <select statement>
```

Creates a view (acts as logical table)

```
create index <index_name> on <table_name> (index_column_name, ...)
```

Creates index on columns of table (increases the speed of data retrieval)

```
alter table <table_name> <alter_specification>
```

where `<alter_specification>` specifies the alternations which are to be done on the table, include

```
add column <column_name> <column_specification>
add index <index_name> (index_column_name, ...)
modify column column_name column_definition
drop column column_name
disable keys
enable keys
```

Alters the definition of an existing table

```
alter view <view_name> [(column_names)] as <select statement>
```

Alters the definition of an existing view

```
drop database <database_name>
```

Drops the specified database (all the tables in that database will be dropped automatically)

```
drop index <index_name> on <table_name>
```

Drops the specified index from the specified table

```
drop table <table_name>
```

Drops the table from the database (all the records in that table will be deleted automatically)

```
drop view <view_name>
```

Drops the specified view

Data manipulation commands:

```
insert into <table_name> (column_names)
      values (comma_spearated_values_for_columns)

insert into <table_name> (column_names) <select_statement>
```

Inserts data into the specified database table

```
update <table_name> set column_name = value, ... [where condition]
```

Updates specified values with specified columns of the specified table

```
delete from <table_name> [where condition]
```

Deletes record(s) from the specified database table

```
select [distinct] column_names from <table_name> [where condition]
```

Selects the specified columns from the specified database table. The symbol '*' represents all the columns in the database table. A special table named 'DUAL' can be used where no tables are referred.

```
truncate table <table_name>
```

Deletes all the records in the specified database table, only table structure remains. Even though it looks similar to deleting all records using DELETE statement. Differences are many, which include the following.

Some DB Structures of MySQL (for example, InnoDB) drops and recreates the table, instead of deleting rows (while there are no foreign key references). This is very fast approach, especially truncating table with huge data. The `AUTO_INCREMENT` (identity column) will be reset while truncating.

And "`ON DELETE`" trigger will not be fired while truncating a table.

Transaction commands:

```
start transaction
```

Begins a new transaction (a group of operations)

```
commit
```

Commit the current transaction, as the result all the changes done in the transaction will become permanent

```
savepoint <savepoint-identifier>
```

Defines a savepoint (marker) in a transaction. Start the transaction before using savepoint.

```
rollback
```

Rolls back the current transaction (cancel the changes).

The following syntax rolls back up to the defined savepoint.

```
rollback to savepoint <savepoint-identifier>
```

Administration-oriented commands:

```
create user <user_id> [identified by 'password']
```

Creates a user with the specified password. The square brackets [ ] represents password is optional.

```
drop user <user_name>
```

Removes the specified user

```
rename user <user_id> to <new_user_id>
```

Renames existing user id to the specified user id

```
set password [for <user_id>] = password('password')
```

Sets (new) password for the specified user. The part [for <user_id>] is required when setting password from 'root' user.

```
grant privilege_type on table|function|procedure
   *.* | db_name.* | db_name.table_name |dbname.functionname ...
   to <user> [with grant option]
```

Some of the privilege_type are as follows.

```
ALL, CREATE,  ALTER, CREATE ROUTINE, ALTER ROUTINE, CREATE USER,
CREATE VIEW, UPDATE, DELETE, DROP, INSERT, SELECT, TRIGGER
```

Grants privileges to users

```
revoke privilege_type on table|function|procedure
    *.* | db_name.* | db_name.table_name |dbname.functionname ...
    from <user>
```

Revokes privileges from users.

The following statement revokes all the privileges from the specified user and his 'grant option' also revoked (which enables the user to grant privileges to other users on the specified objects).

```
revoke all privileges, grant option from user
```

```
show tables
```

Displays all the tables in the connected database

```
show triggers
```

Displays all the triggers currently defined for tables in the connected database

```
show variables
```

Displays all the variables defined for the user. Use SET statement to set/change value of a variable. For example, the following statement makes all foreign-key checking to be off.

```
set foreign_key_checks = 0
```

`show databases`	Displays all the databases on the MySQL server host
desc <table_name>	Describes the specified table (information about the table)
`show triggers`	Displays all the triggers currently defined for tables in the connected database
`show triggers`	Displays all the triggers currently defined for tables in the connected database

3.6 MySQL STORAGE ENGINES

These storage engines (table types) act as handlers for different types of tables in database, which supports transaction, locking, etc. We can decide which storage engine is very much opt for our data. Default storage engine is MyISAM. Some of the preferable storage engines are given below.

MyISAM:

It stores data on disks and it is well suited for low overhead database operations and it does not support transactions.

InnoDB:

It stores data on disks and it is transaction-safe storage engine that supports transactions (commit/rollback). This storage engine requires more disk spaces to store data when compared with MyISAM.

Memory:

It stores data on primary memory (RAM), of course the data will be deleted when system became down/crash. It provides very fast access to data.

CSV:

It stores data on text files using Comma Separated Values (CSV) format. Since this CSV format is more understandable by all the applications, it is easy to exchange data among applications.

Use "show engines" command to get list of supported storage engines of you MySQL version.

We can set the storage engine for a table at the time of creation by suffixing the following phrase.

```
engine = <storage_engine_name>
```

Example:

```
create table <table_name> (<column_definitions>) engine = innodb;
```

We can also set a storage engine for already existing table as below:

```
alter table <table_name> engine = <storage_engine_name>
```

3.7 MySQL PROGRAMS

These programs are provided by MySQL, which are used for specialised functions. In this section, only two important programs (mysql and mysqldump) are explained.

mysql:

This program is used to connect to MySQL and provides command-based user interface.

On the command prompt (DOS Window / Shell), invoke the mysql program to make connection with MySQL.

Typical format

```
mysql –h <server_host_of_mysql> -u <user_id> -p<password> <database_
      schema>
```

It connect to the MySQL server, which is running in the specified host (default to localhost) using the specified user_id and password. The specified database_schema will be opened and used for the current session. Note that you should not give any space between –p option and the password.

mysqldump:

It is a command-line interface, which is used to dump (Backup) database(s).

To dump specific tables:

```
mysqldump -u <user_id> -p<password>
                    <database_schema> <table_name1> <table_name2> ...
```

To dump specific databases:

```
mysqldump -u <user_id> -p<password>
                 --databases <database_schema1> <database_schema2> ...
```

To dump all databases:

```
mysqldump -u <user_id> -p<password>  --all-databases
```

Generally root user-id is specified while dumping all databases, because the root user has rights on all databases.

Usually, the database dump (backup) is generated as SQL statements. We can change the settings to store in some other formats such as CSV (Comma Separated Values).

The following are some of the options that can be used with mysqld.

Option	Description
-u <user_name>	User name to connect to the server
-p<password>	Password to connect to the server
-h <MySQL_server_host>	Dumps from the specified host (computer), where MySQL is running
--all-databases (or) –A	Dumps all databases.
--databases <database_names> (or) –B <database_names>	Adds specified databases

Option	Description
`--no-create-db` (or) `-n`	Suppresses (does not include) the CREATE DATABASE statements for dumping.
`--no-create-info` (or) `-t`	Suppresses CREATE TABLE statements.
`--no-data` (or) `-d`	Suppresses INSERT statements (does not dump records of tables)
`--add-drop-database`	Includes DROP DATABASE statements before CREATE DATABASE statements.
`--add-drop-table`	Includes DROP TABLE statements before CREATE TABLE statements.
`--complete-insert`	Uses complete INSERT statement including column-names for dumping.
`--extended-insert` (or) `–e`	Use single INSERT statement for dumping all the records of a table.
`--skip-extended-insert`	Uses separate INSERT statement for each record in the table. Extended insert uses single INSERT statement with multiple records (records are separated by commas).
`--quick` (or) `–q`	It outputs each row (dump to screen) immediately when it is received and avoids caching of rows before dump. While dumping tables with huge data, inadequate cache problem may occur as MySQL caches rows of entire row set before outputting (dumping). In this case, this option is useful which forces this program to retrieve one row at a time from the server for a table, rather than retrieving the entire row set and buffering it in memory before dumping.
`--force` (or) `–f`	Forces to continue dumping even if SQL errors occurred during dump process. Normally, dump process will be exited when an SQL error occurred.
`--add-locks`	Includes LOCK TABLES statement before each table dump and UNLOCK TABLES statement after each table dump.
`--routines` (or) `–R`	Dumps stored routines (procedures and functions).
`--triggers`	Dumps triggers for each dumped table. This is enabled by default. Use -- skip-triggers to disable it.

`--opt`	This is a shorthand option for group of options:
	`--add-drop-table --add-locks --create-options`
	`--disable-keys --extended-insert --lock-tables`
	`--quick --set-charset`
	By default, this option is enabled. Use --- skip-opt to disable it.

`--comments` (or) `-i`	Writes additional information in the dump files such as server version, server host, etc.
`--xml`	Uses XML format for dumping.

Dumping and Restoring:

Redirect the dump output into file.

```
mysqldump attribute_options > dumpfile
```

The above statement redirects the dump output to a file named "dumpfile".

To restore the dump to MySQL (at any host), use the following syntax (on command / shell prompt)

```
mysql < dumpfile
```

3.8 BUILT-IN FUNCTIONS

MySQL provides rich set of built-in functions. Some of them are given below:

Numeric functions:

`abs(value)`	Returns the absolute value. abs(10) = 10, abs(-10) = 10
`ceil(value)`	Returns the smallest integer value that is greater than or equal to the specified value
`floor(value)`	Returns the largest number that is less than or equal to the specified value
`pow(x,y)`	Returns x^y (the value of x raised to the power of y)
`sqrt(value)`	Returns the square root of the specified value
`mod(dividend, divisor)`	Returns modulo value of dividend/divisor
`round(value, decimal_places)`	Rounds the specified value to the specified decimal_places. A fractional value >= 0.5 will be rounded up to the nearest integer.
`truncate(value, decimal_places)`	Returns the specified value to the specified decimal-places; however the value will not be rounded up/down.

String functions:

`char(value)`	Returns character of the specified ASCII value
`concat(string1, string2)`	Returns the concatenation of string1 and string2
`format(value, digits)`	Formats the specified value in '#,###.#' with 'digits' after decimal point. Value will be rounded up to nearest value while decimal places shrinking due to fewer digits specified.

`length(string)`	Returns the length of string in bytes
`lower(string)`	Returns the string in lower-case
`upper(string)`	Returns the string in upper-case
`ltrim(string)`	Returns the string with leading spaces are removed
`rtrim(string)`	Returns the string with trailing spaces are removed
`trim(string)`	Returns the string with leading and trailing spaces are removed
`substring(string, offset, length)`	Returns substring of string starting from offset (starts with 1) and 'length' number of characters. A negative offset searches for substring from right to left of string.
`locate(search_string, string)`	Searches search_string in string and returns the offset of first match in the string, returns "0" if there is no match found.
`replace(string, from_string, to_string)`	Returns the "string" with all the occurrences of "from_string" is replaced by "to_string"
`reverse(string)`	Returns the "string" reversed
`strcmp(string1, string2)`	Returns 0, if both strings are equal. Returns -1, if string1 is less than the string2 (ASCII comparison) Returns 1, if string1 is greater than the string2

Date and time functions:

`curdate()`	Returns the system date (in YYYY-MM-DD format) (%Y-%m-%d)
`curtime()`	Returns the system time (in HH:MI:SS format) (%k-%i-%s)
`sysdate()`	Returns the system date and time
`adddate(date, days)`	Returns the date with specified days are added
`subdate(date, days)`	Returns the date with specified days are subtracted
`addtime(time1, time2)`	Returns time1 with time2 is added. Usually, time is specified in 'HH24:MI:SS' format/'HH24:MI:SS.Microseconds' format
`subtime(time1, time2)`	Returns time1 with time2 is subtracted
`date_format(date, format)`	Returns date in specified format. The '%' character should be prefixed to every format specifier.

%a	Abbreviated day name (Sun, Mon, ... Sat)
%b	Abbreviated month name (Jan, Feb, ... Dec)
%W	Day name (Sunday, Monday, ... Saturday)
%M	Month name (January, February, ... December)
%Y	Year (YYYY)
%y	Year (YY)
%m	Month (MM) valid month: 01 to 12
%c	Month (M) valid month: 1 to 12
%d	Day of the month (DD) 00 to 31
%e	Day of the month (D) 0 to 31
%H	Hour (HH24) 00 to 23
%h	Hour (HH) 01 to 12 (00 will be displayed as 12)
%i	Minutes (MI) 00 to 59
%S	Seconds (SS) 00 to 59
%f	Microseconds 000000 to 999999
%p	AM, PM

`str_to_date(date_in_string, date_format)`	Returns the date of the specified `date_in_string`. The `date_format` is for specifying in what format date is present in `date_in_string`.
`date(date)`	Returns the date part (YYYY-MM-DD) of specified date
`year(date)`	Returns the year part of the specified date
`month(date)`	Returns the month part of the specified date
`day(date)`	Returns the day part of the specified date
`hour(time/date_time)`	Returns the hour part of the specified time/date_time
`minute (time/date_time)`	Returns the minutes part of the specified time/date_time
`second (time/date_time)`	Returns the second part of the specified time/date_time
`microsecond(time/date_time)`	Returns the microseconds part of the specified time/date_time
`datediff(date1, date2)`	Returns date difference between date1 and date2 (date1 – date2) in days

Aggregate functions:

`count(*)`	Returns the total number of records (that the query retrieves)
`count(distinct column-name)`	Returns the total number of different (distinct) values of the specified column
`sum(column_name)`	Returns the summation of values in the specified column
`avg(column_name)`	Returns the average of the values in the specified column
`max(column_name)`	Returns the maximum value in the specified column
`min(column_name)`	Returns the minimum value in the specified column

Miscellaneous session related functions:

`user()`	Returns currently logged user name and host-name
`version()`	Returns the MySQL version

3.9 PL/SQL

The PL/SQL (Procedural Language/Structured Query Language) is a procedural extension (supports decision making, looping, functions/procedures, etc.) of SQL.

3.9.1 Conditional Constructs

Statements in a block should be terminated by semi-colon.

if statement:

Format I

```
if <condition> then
    statements
end if
```

Format II

```
if <condition> then
    statements
else
    statements
end if
```

Format III

```
if <condition> then
    statements
elseif <condition> then
    statements
...
else
    statements
end if
```

case statement:

Format I

```
case value
  when value1 then statements
  when value2 then statements
  ...
  else statements
end case
```

Format II

```
case
  when condition1 then statements
  when condition2 then statements
  ...
  else statements
end case
```

3.9.2 Iterative Statements

loop statement:

```
<label>: loop
        statements
    end loop <label>
```

Both the label name should be same. The above format results in an infinite loop. Use LEAVE statement which is used to come out of a loop.

```
LEAVE <loop_label>
```

while loop:

This is an entry-controlled loop; the body of the loop will be executed as long as the condition becomes true.

Simple while loop

```
while <condition> do
   statements
end while
```

while loop with label

```
<label>: while <condition> do
            statements
            leave <label>
         end while <label>
```

repeat..until loop:

This is an exit-controlled loop; the body of the loop will be executed first time with out checking any condition and executed as long as the condition becomes true.

Simple repeat..until loop

```
repeat
   statements
   until  <condition>
end repeat
```

repeat..until loop with label

```
<label>: repeat
            statements
            until  <condition>
         end repeat <label>
```

The iterate statement continues the loop execution without executing remaining statements after iterate in the loop. Thus, this statement is used to skip one iteration.

General format

```
iterate <label>
```

3.9.3 Cursors

A Cursor is a database object, which is used to traverse the results of an SQL query.

Declaring cursor:

```
declare <cursor_name> cursor for <select_statement>
```

Opening cursor:

```
open <cursor_name>
```

Fetching data from cursor:

This statement fetches one row (if exists) from the cursor pointer and automatically moves the cursor pointer to next row (if exists).

```
fetch <cursor_name> into variable_name1, variable_name2, ...
```

Closing a cursor:

```
close <cursor_name>
```

3.9.4 Triggers

A trigger is a database object (usually in the format of stored procedure) associated with a table and invoked automatically when a predefined event occurs on the table.

General format to create a trigger

```
create trigger <trigger_name>
before|after
insert|update|delete
on <table_name>
for each row
<trigger_statements>
```

The two special keywords OLD and NEW are used to access the data on the table before and after the triggered event takes place. The notation `OLD.column_name` refers the value of the column_name of an existing row (in case of `UPDATE/DELETE`) and `NEW.column_name` refers the value of the value is to be inserted / updated. The "`FOR EACH ROW`" makes the trigger to fire once for each row of the table (on which the trigger is set) is affected.

3.9.5 Stored Procedures

A stored procedure is a set of SQL statements with conditional constructs that has been compiled and stored on the database server. The Stored procedures are similar to functions/methods/procedures in high-level programming languages such as C, Java, and Visual Basic.

A stored-procedure may return one or many values, or even no value.

General format

```
create procedure <procedure_name>(IN|OUT|INOUT parameter-name data-type,
    ...)
Procedure_Body
```

The Procedure_Body may contain compound statement which is enclosed by BEGIN and END keywords.

```
begin
    statements
end
```

A compound statement can contain multiple statements separated by semicolon and it can contain other compound statements.

Declaring local variables:

```
declare variable_name1, variable_name2, ... data-type [default value]
```

Assigning values to variables:

```
set variable_name1 = value, variable_name2 = value2, ...
```

Parameters:

`IN`: This is default parameter. It is passed to calling procedure by caller and can be used in the procedure. Any change on this type of parameter will not be reflected in the caller.

`OUT`: This type of parameter is used to pass the value from called procedure to caller.

`INOUT`: This type of parameter is passed by the caller to calling procedure and it can be used in the procedure. Any change on this variable will also be reflected in the caller.

Calling a stored procedure:

General format

```
call <procedure_name>(parameters)
```

Dropping a stored procedure:

General format

```
drop procedure <procedure_name>
```

3.9.6 Stored Functions

Functions must return one value and only one.

General format

```
create function <function_name>(parameters) returns <data_type_of_return_
    value>
Function_Body
```

A `RETURN` statement terminates the execution of a stored function and returns a value to the caller. There may be more `RETURN` statement with in a function (multiple return point), but at least one.

Use `OUT/INOUT` type parameters to get values (return values) from the called procedure.

Calling a stored function:

```
function_name(parameters)
```

Use assignment statement to store the returned value from a function into a variable.

Dropping a stored function:

General format:

```
drop function <stored_function_name>
```

Note: On writing stored procedures/functions: MySQL uses semicolon as standard statement delimiter. As a procedure/function may use compound statements (made up of several statements separated by semicolon), MySQL interpret the semicolon wrongly and unwanted result/ error will appear. To overcome this issue, change MySQL standard delimiter to some other character (other than semi-colon) using DELIMITER statement. After the execution of the stored procedure/function, change the MySQL standard delimiter to semicolon. This setting is only required at the time of defining (compiling) procedures/functions, not at the time of calling.

The following example changes MySQL standard delimiter to '//' before compiling stored procedure.

```
delimiter //
create procedure <procedure_name>(parameters)
begin
    <statements>
end//
delimiter ;
```

3.10 ILLUSTRATING EXAMPLES

Creating a Table

```
mysql> create table student (rno int, sname varchar(15), m1 int, m2 int);
    Query OK, 0 rows affected (0.10 sec)
mysql> desc student;
+-------+-------------+------+-----+---------+-------+
| Field | Type        | Null | Key | Default | Extra |
+-------+-------------+------+-----+---------+-------+
| rno   | int(11)     | YES  |     | NULL    |       |
| sname | varchar(15) | YES  |     | NULL    |       |
| m1    | int(11)     | YES  |     | NULL    |       |
| m2    | int(11)     | YES  |     | NULL    |       |
+-------+-------------+------+-----+---------+-------+
4 rows in set (0.03 sec)
```

Altering a Table

```
mysql> alter table student add (m3 int, total int, result char(4));
Query OK, 0 rows affected (0.16 sec)
Records: 0  Duplicates: 0  Warnings: 0

mysql> desc student;
+--------+-------------+------+-----+---------+-------+
| Field  | Type        | Null | Key | Default | Extra |
+--------+-------------+------+-----+---------+-------+
| rno    | int(11)     | YES  |     | NULL    |       |
| sname  | varchar(15) | YES  |     | NULL    |       |
| m1     | int(11)     | YES  |     | NULL    |       |
| m2     | int(11)     | YES  |     | NULL    |       |
| m3     | int(11)     | YES  |     | NULL    |       |
| total  | int(11)     | YES  |     | NULL    |       |
| result | char(4)     | YES  |     | NULL    |       |
+--------+-------------+------+-----+---------+-------+
7 rows in set (0.00 sec)
```

```
mysql> alter table student modify result varchar(4);
Query OK, 0 rows affected (0.20 sec)
Records: 0  Duplicates: 0  Warnings: 0
mysql> desc student;
+--------+-------------+------+-----+---------+-------+
| Field  | Type        | Null | Key | Default | Extra |
+--------+-------------+------+-----+---------+-------+
| rno    | int(11)     | YES  |     | NULL    |       |
| sname  | varchar(15) | YES  |     | NULL    |       |
| m1     | int(11)     | YES  |     | NULL    |       |
| m2     | int(11)     | YES  |     | NULL    |       |
| m3     | int(11)     | YES  |     | NULL    |       |
| total  | int(11)     | YES  |     | NULL    |       |
| result | varchar(4)  | YES  |     | NULL    |       |
+--------+-------------+------+-----+---------+-------+
7 rows in set (0.00 sec)
```

Dropping a Table

```
mysql> drop table student;
Query OK, 0 rows affected (0.02 sec)

mysql> desc student;
ERROR 1146 (42S02): Table 'demodb.student' doesn't exist
```

Integrity Constraints

```
mysql> create table stud (rno int primary key, sname varchar(15) not
    null);
Query OK, 0 rows affected (0.05 sec)

mysql> desc stud;
+-------+-------------+------+-----+---------+-------+
| Field | Type        | Null | Key | Default | Extra |
+-------+-------------+------+-----+---------+-------+
| rno   | int(11)     | NO   | PRI | NULL    |       |
| sname | varchar(15) | NO   |     | NULL    |       |
+-------+-------------+------+-----+---------+-------+
2 rows in set (0.00 sec)

mysql> insert into stud (rno, sname) values (1001, 'Ibrahim');
Query OK, 1 row affected (0.04 sec)

mysql> insert into stud (rno, sname) values (1002, 'Ibrahim');
Query OK, 1 row affected (0.02 sec)
```

```
mysql> select * from stud;
+------+---------+
| rno  | sname   |
+------+---------+
| 1001 | Ibrahim |
| 1002 | Ibrahim |
+------+---------+
2 rows in set (0.00 sec)
```

Attempting to insert already existing value '1002' for primary key column (rno),

```
mysql> insert into stud (rno, sname) values (1002, 'Ameer');
ERROR 1062 (23000): Duplicate entry '1002' for key 'PRIMARY'
```

Attempting to insert 'null' value for 'not null' column (sname),

```
mysql> insert into stud (rno, sname) values (1002, null);
ERROR 1048 (23000): Column 'sname' cannot be null
```

Inserting Values

```
mysql> desc student;
+--------+-------------+------+-----+---------+-------+
| Field  | Type        | Null | Key | Default | Extra |
+--------+-------------+------+-----+---------+-------+
| rno    | int(11)     | YES  |     | NULL    |       |
| sname  | varchar(15) | YES  |     | NULL    |       |
| m1     | int(11)     | YES  |     | NULL    |       |
| m2     | int(11)     | YES  |     | NULL    |       |
| m3     | int(11)     | YES  |     | NULL    |       |
| total  | int(11)     | YES  |     | NULL    |       |
| result | varchar(4)  | YES  |     | NULL    |       |
+--------+-------------+------+-----+---------+-------+
7 rows in set (0.00 sec)

mysql> insert into student (rno, sname, m1, m2, m3) values
    ->                        (1001, 'IBRAHIM', 60, 70, 80);
Query OK, 1 row affected (0.03 sec)

mysql> insert into student (rno, sname, m1, m2, m3) values
    ->                        (1002, 'KUMAR', 65, 86, 92);
Query OK, 1 row affected (0.03 sec)

mysql> insert into student (rno, sname, m1, m2, m3) values
    ->                        (1003, 'RAHMAN', 49, 50, 55);
```

```
Query OK, 1 row affected (0.02 sec)

mysql> select * from student;
+------+---------+------+------+------+-------+--------+
| rno  | sname   | m1   | m2   | m3   | total | result |
+------+---------+------+------+------+-------+--------+
| 1001 | IBRAHIM |   60 |   70 |   80 |  NULL | NULL   |
| 1002 | KUMAR   |   65 |   86 |   92 |  NULL | NULL   |
| 1003 | RAHMAN  |   49 |   50 |   55 |  NULL | NULL   |
+------+---------+------+------+------+-------+--------+
3 rows in set (0.00 sec)
```

Updating data in a table

```
mysql> update student set total = m1 + m2 + m3;
Query OK, 3 rows affected (0.03 sec)
Rows matched: 3  Changed: 3  Warnings: 0

mysql> update student set result='PASS' where m1 >= 50 and m2 >= 50 and
    m3 >= 50;
Query OK, 2 rows affected (0.03 sec)
Rows matched: 2  Changed: 2  Warnings: 0

mysql> update student set result='FAIL' where m1 < 50 or m2 < 50 or m3 < 50;
Query OK, 1 row affected (0.02 sec)
Rows matched: 1  Changed: 1  Warnings: 0
```

Selecting data from a table

```
mysql> select * from student;
+------+---------+------+------+------+-------+--------+
| rno  | sname   | m1   | m2   | m3   | total | result |
+------+---------+------+------+------+-------+--------+
| 1001 | IBRAHIM |   60 |   70 |   80 |   210 | PASS   |
| 1002 | KUMAR   |   65 |   86 |   92 |   243 | PASS   |
| 1003 | RAHMAN  |   49 |   50 |   55 |   154 | FAIL   |
+------+---------+------+------+------+-------+--------+
3 rows in set (0.00 sec)

mysql> select rno, result from student;
+------+--------+
| rno  | result |
+------+--------+
| 1001 | PASS   |
```

```
| 1002 | PASS   |
| 1003 | FAIL   |
+------+--------+
3 rows in set (0.00 sec)

mysql> select * from student where rno=1002;
+------+-------+------+------+------+-------+--------+
| rno  | sname | m1   | m2   | m3   | total | result |
+------+-------+------+------+------+-------+--------+
| 1002 | KUMAR |   65 |   86 |   92 |   243 | PASS   |
+------+-------+------+------+------+-------+--------+
1 row in set (0.00 sec)

mysql> select * from student where result='PASS';
+------+---------+------+------+------+-------+--------+
| rno  | sname   | m1   | m2   | m3   | total | result |
+------+---------+------+------+------+-------+--------+
| 1001 | IBRAHIM |   60 |   70 |   80 |   210 | PASS   |
| 1002 | KUMAR   |   65 |   86 |   92 |   243 | PASS   |
+------+---------+------+------+------+-------+--------+
2 rows in set (0.00 sec)
```

Deleting rows from a table

```
mysql> select * from student;
+------+---------+------+------+------+-------+--------+
| rno  | sname   | m1   | m2   | m3   | total | result |
+------+---------+------+------+------+-------+--------+
| 1001 | IBRAHIM |   60 |   70 |   80 |   210 | PASS   |
| 1002 | KUMAR   |   65 |   86 |   92 |   243 | PASS   |
| 1003 | RAHMAN  |   49 |   50 |   55 |   154 | FAIL   |
+------+---------+------+------+------+-------+--------+
3 rows in set (0.00 sec)

mysql> delete from student where rno=1002;
Query OK, 1 row affected (0.03 sec)

mysql> select * from student;
+------+---------+------+------+------+-------+--------+
| rno  | sname   | m1   | m2   | m3   | total | result |
+------+---------+------+------+------+-------+--------+
| 1001 | IBRAHIM |   60 |   70 |   80 |   210 | PASS   |
| 1003 | RAHMAN  |   49 |   50 |   55 |   154 | FAIL   |
+------+---------+------+------+------+-------+--------+
2 rows in set (0.00 sec)
```

```
mysql> truncate student;
Query OK, 0 rows affected (0.02 sec)

mysql> select * from student;
Empty set (0.00 sec)
```

Performing a Transaction

```
mysql> create table stud (rno int, result varchar(6));
Query OK, 0 rows affected (0.06 sec)

mysql> insert into stud values (1001, 'PASS');
Query OK, 1 row affected (0.03 sec)

mysql> insert into stud values (1002, 'FAIL');
Query OK, 1 row affected (0.02 sec)

mysql> insert into stud values (1003, 'PASS');
Query OK, 1 row affected (0.03 sec)

mysql> select * from stud;
+------+--------+
| rno  | result |
+------+--------+
| 1001 | PASS   |
| 1002 | FAIL   |
| 1003 | PASS   |
+------+--------+
3 rows in set (0.00 sec)

mysql> commit;
Query OK, 0 rows affected (0.00 sec)

mysql> select * from stud;
+------+--------+
| rno  | result |
+------+--------+
| 1001 | PASS   |
| 1002 | FAIL   |
| 1003 | PASS   |
+------+--------+
3 rows in set (0.00 sec)
```

```
mysql> start transaction;
Query OK, 0 rows affected (0.00 sec)

mysql> update stud set result='PASS' where rno=1002;
Query OK, 1 row affected (0.00 sec)
Rows matched: 1  Changed: 1  Warnings: 0

mysql> select * from stud;
+------+--------+
| rno  | result |
+------+--------+
| 1001 | PASS   |
| 1002 | PASS   |
| 1003 | PASS   |
+------+--------+
3 rows in set (0.00 sec)

mysql> savepoint sp;
Query OK, 0 rows affected (0.00 sec)

mysql> update stud set result='FAIL' where rno=1001;
Query OK, 1 row affected (0.00 sec)
Rows matched: 1  Changed: 1  Warnings: 0

mysql> update stud set result='FAIL' where rno=1003;
Query OK, 1 row affected (0.00 sec)
Rows matched: 1  Changed: 1  Warnings: 0

mysql> select * from stud;
+------+--------+
| rno  | result |
+------+--------+
| 1001 | FAIL   |
| 1002 | PASS   |
| 1003 | FAIL   |
+------+--------+
3 rows in set (0.00 sec)

mysql> rollback to savepoint sp;
Query OK, 0 rows affected (0.00 sec)
```

```
mysql> select * from stud;
+------+--------+
| rno  | result |
+------+--------+
| 1001 | PASS   |
| 1002 | PASS   |
| 1003 | PASS   |
+------+--------+
3 rows in set (0.00 sec)

mysql> rollback;
Query OK, 0 rows affected (0.03 sec)

mysql> select * from stud;
+------+--------+
| rno  | result |
+------+--------+
| 1001 | PASS   |
| 1002 | FAIL   |
| 1003 | PASS   |
+------+--------+
3 rows in set (0.00 sec)
```

Set operations

MySQL supports UNION directly, not INTERSECTION and MINUS (we have to use JOIN operation).

```
mysql> select * from stud1;
+------+--------+
| rno  | result |
+------+--------+
| 1001 | PASS   |
| 1002 | FAIL   |
| 1003 | PASS   |
+------+--------+
3 rows in set (0.00 sec)

mysql> select * from stud2;
+------+--------+
| rno  | result |
+------+--------+
| 1001 | PASS   |
| 1004 | FAIL   |
+------+--------+
2 rows in set (0.00 sec)
```

```
mysql> select * from stud1 union select * from stud2;
+------+--------+
| rno  | result |
+------+--------+
| 1001 | PASS   |
| 1002 | FAIL   |
| 1003 | PASS   |
| 1004 | FAIL   |
+------+--------+
4 rows in set (0.00 sec)

mysql> select * from stud1 union all select * from stud2;
+------+--------+
| rno  | result |
+------+--------+
| 1001 | PASS   |
| 1002 | FAIL   |
| 1003 | PASS   |
| 1001 | PASS   |
| 1004 | FAIL   |
+------+--------+
5 rows in set (0.00 sec)
```

Intersection set operation using inner join:

```
mysql> select * from stud1
    -> inner join stud2 using (rno, result);
+------+--------+
| rno  | result |
+------+--------+
| 1001 | PASS   |
+------+--------+
1 row in set (0.00 sec)
```

Minus set operation using left join

```
mysql> select distinct * from stud1
    -> left join stud2 using (rno, result)
    -> where stud2.rno is null;
```

```
+------+--------+
| rno  | result |
+------+--------+
| 1002 | FAIL   |
| 1003 | PASS   |
+------+--------+
2 rows in set (0.01 sec)

mysql> select stud1.* from stud1
    -> left join stud2 on stud1.rno = stud2.rno
    -> where stud2.rno is null;
+------+--------+
| rno  | result |
+------+--------+
| 1002 | FAIL   |
| 1003 | PASS   |
+------+--------+
2 rows in set (0.00 sec)
```

Join Operations:

```
mysql> create table st1 (rno int, sname varchar(15));
Query OK, 0 rows affected (0.16 sec)

mysql> create table st2 (rno int, total int, result varchar(4));
Query OK, 0 rows affected (0.09 sec)

mysql> insert into st1 (rno, sname) values
    -> (1000, 'Ibrahim'), (1001, 'Kannan'), (1003, 'Navas');
Query OK, 3 rows affected (0.06 sec)
Records: 3  Duplicates: 0  Warnings: 0

mysql> insert into st2 (rno, total, result) values
    -> (1000, 234, 'Pass'), (1001, 123, 'Fail'), (1002, 290, 'Pass');
Query OK, 3 rows affected (0.05 sec)
Records: 3  Duplicates: 0  Warnings: 0

mysql> select * from st1;
+------+---------+
| rno  | sname   |
+------+---------+
| 1000 | Ibrahim |
| 1001 | Kannan  |
| 1003 | Navas   |
+------+---------+
3 rows in set (0.00 sec)
```

```
mysql> select * from st2;
+------+-------+--------+
| rno  | total | result |
+------+-------+--------+
| 1000 |   234 | Pass   |
| 1001 |   123 | Fail   |
| 1002 |   290 | Pass   |
+------+-------+--------+
3 rows in set (0.00 sec)

mysql> select st1.rno, st1.sname, st2.result
    ->          from st1, st2 where st1.rno=st2.rno;
+------+---------+--------+
| rno  | sname   | result |
+------+---------+--------+
| 1000 | Ibrahim | Pass   |
| 1001 | Kannan  | Fail   |
+------+---------+--------+
2 rows in set (0.00 sec)
```

```
Left outer join
     mysql> select * from st1 left outer join st2 on st1.rno = st2.rno;
     +------+---------+------+-------+--------+
     | rno  | sname   | rno  | total | result |
     +------+---------+------+-------+--------+
     | 1000 | Ibrahim | 1000 |   234 | Pass   |
     | 1001 | Kannan  | 1001 |   123 | Fail   |
     | 1003 | Navas   | NULL |  NULL | NULL   |
     +------+---------+------+-------+--------+
     3 rows in set (0.05 sec)
```

This query retrieves the rows which has the same rno value in both tables and also retrieves rows which are unique to st1 (unmatched rows of st1). This join is also called as "Left Outer Join".

```
Right Outer Join
     mysql> select * from st1 right outer join st2 on st1.rno = st2.rno;
     +------+---------+------+-------+--------+
     | rno  | sname   | rno  | total | result |
     +------+---------+------+-------+--------+
     | 1000 | Ibrahim | 1000 |   234 | Pass   |
     | 1001 | Kannan  | 1001 |   123 | Fail   |
     | NULL | NULL    | 1002 |   290 | Pass   |
     +------+---------+------+-------+--------+
     3 rows in set (0.00 sec)
```

This query retrieves the rows which has the same rno value in both tables and also retrieves rows which are unique to st2 (unmatched rows of st2). This process is also called as "Right Outer Join".

Sub-queries:

A query may contain another query for simplifying its operation, i.e., nesting of such queries one with in another is called sub-query. The sub-queries are written with in parenthesis.

```
mysql> select rno from st2 where total = (select max(total) from st2);
+------+
| rno  |
+------+
| 1002 |
+------+
1 row in set (0.00 sec)
```

Views:

A View may be considered as a logical table. The table(s) upon which a view is based are called as *"base table(s)"*. The views can be accessed like normal tables; any change performed on a view will also be reflected on base table(s) and vice versa.

```
mysql> create table student
    -> (rollnum    int primary key,
    ->  first_name varchar(15),
    ->  last_name  varchar(15)
    -> );
Query OK, 0 rows affected (0.09 sec)

mysql> create table mark
    -> (rollnum    int primary key,
    ->  mark1      int,
    ->  mark2      int
    -> );
Query OK, 0 rows affected (0.11 sec)

mysql> insert into student (rollnum, first_name, last_name) values
    -> (1001, 'Mohamed', 'Ibrahim'), (1002, 'Karan', 'Singh');
Query OK, 2 rows affected (0.05 sec)
Records: 2  Duplicates: 0  Warnings: 0

mysql> insert into mark (rollnum, mark1, mark2) values
    -> (1001, 90, 80), (1002, 10, 20);
Query OK, 2 rows affected (0.06 sec)
Records: 2  Duplicates: 0  Warnings: 0
```

```
mysql> create view student_view as
    -> select s.rollnum, s.first_name, m.mark1 from student s, mark m
    -> where s.rollnum = m.rollnum;
Query OK, 0 rows affected (0.05 sec)

mysql> select * from student;
+---------+------------+-----------+
| rollnum | first_name | last_name |
+---------+------------+-----------+
|    1001 | Mohamed    | Ibrahim   |
|    1002 | Karan      | Singh     |
+---------+------------+-----------+
2 rows in set (0.00 sec)

mysql> select * from mark;
+---------+-------+-------+
| rollnum | mark1 | mark2 |
+---------+-------+-------+
|    1001 |    90 |    80 |
|    1002 |    10 |    20 |
+---------+-------+-------+
2 rows in set (0.00 sec)

mysql> select * from student_view;
+---------+------------+-------+
| rollnum | first_name | mark1 |
+---------+------------+-------+
|    1001 | Mohamed    |    90 |
|    1002 | Karan      |    10 |
+---------+------------+-------+
2 rows in set (0.02 sec)

mysql> delete from mark where rollnum = 1001;
Query OK, 1 row affected (0.05 sec)

mysql> select * from student_view;
+---------+------------+-------+
| rollnum | first_name | mark1 |
+---------+------------+-------+
|    1002 | Karan      |    10 |
+---------+------------+-------+
1 row in set (0.02 sec)
```

```
mysql> insert into student (rollnum, first_name, last_name)
    -> values (1003, 'Ravi', 'Chandren');
Query OK, 1 row affected (0.05 sec)

mysql> insert into mark (rollnum, mark1, mark2) values (1003, 50, 60);
Query OK, 1 row affected (0.06 sec)

mysql> select * from student_view;
+---------+------------+-------+
| rollnum | first_name | mark1 |
+---------+------------+-------+
|    1002 | Karan      |    10 |
|    1003 | Ravi       |    50 |
+---------+------------+-------+
2 rows in set (0.00 sec)

mysql> update mark set mark1 = mark1 + 5, mark2 = mark2 + 4;
Query OK, 2 rows affected (0.08 sec)
Rows matched: 2  Changed: 2  Warnings: 0

mysql> select * from mark;
+---------+-------+-------+
| rollnum | mark1 | mark2 |
+---------+-------+-------+
|    1002 |    15 |    24 |
|    1003 |    55 |    64 |
+---------+-------+-------+
2 rows in set (0.00 sec)

mysql> select * from student_view;
+---------+------------+-------+
| rollnum | first_name | mark1 |
+---------+------------+-------+
|    1002 | Karan      |    15 |
|    1003 | Ravi       |    55 |
+---------+------------+-------+
2 rows in set (0.00 sec)

mysql> update student_view set mark1 = mark1 + 10;
Query OK, 2 rows affected (0.06 sec)
Rows matched: 2  Changed: 2  Warnings: 0
```

```
mysql> select * from student_view;
+---------+------------+-------+
| rollnum | first_name | mark1 |
+---------+------------+-------+
|    1002 | Karan      |    25 |
|    1003 | Ravi       |    65 |
+---------+------------+-------+
2 rows in set (0.00 sec)

mysql> select * from mark;
+---------+-------+-------+
| rollnum | mark1 | mark2 |
+---------+-------+-------+
|    1002 |    25 |    24 |
|    1003 |    65 |    64 |
+---------+-------+-------+
2 rows in set (0.00 sec)
```

Build-in functions:

Group functions:

```
mysql> create table stud (rno int, mark int);
Query OK, 0 rows affected (0.89 sec)

mysql> insert into stud (rno, mark) values
    -> (1001, 78), (1002,65),(1003,98),(1004,34),(1005,32);
Query OK, 5 rows affected (0.39 sec)
Records: 5  Duplicates: 0  Warnings: 0

mysql> select * from stud;
+------+------+
| rno  | mark |
+------+------+
| 1001 |   78 |
| 1002 |   65 |
| 1003 |   98 |
| 1004 |   34 |
| 1005 |   32 |
+------+------+
5 rows in set (0.58 sec)
```

```
mysql> select sum(mark) from stud;
+-----------+
| sum(mark) |
+-----------+
|       307 |
+-----------+
1 row in set (0.24 sec)

mysql> select max(mark) from stud;
+-----------+
| max(mark) |
+-----------+
|        98 |
+-----------+
1 row in set (0.00 sec)

mysql> select min(mark) from stud;
+-----------+
| min(mark) |
+-----------+
|        32 |
+-----------+
1 row in set (0.05 sec)

mysql> select avg(mark) from stud;
+-----------+
| avg(mark) |
+-----------+
|   61.4000 |
+-----------+
1 row in set (0.00 sec)

mysql> select count(*) from stud;
+----------+
| count(*) |
+----------+
|        5 |
+----------+
1 row in set (0.16 sec)

mysql> select count(mark) from stud;
+-------------+
| count(mark) |
+-------------+
|           5 |
+-------------+
1 row in set (0.00 sec)
```

```
mysql> insert into stud (rno, mark) values
     -> (1006, null);
Query OK, 1 row affected (0.19 sec)

mysql> select * from stud;
+------+------+
| rno  | mark |
+------+------+
| 1001 |   78 |
| 1002 |   65 |
| 1003 |   98 |
| 1004 |   34 |
| 1005 |   32 |
| 1006 | NULL |
+------+------+
6 rows in set (0.00 sec)

mysql> select count(mark) from stud;
+-------------+
| count(mark) |
+-------------+
|           5 |
+-------------+
1 row in set (0.00 sec)

mysql> select count(rno) from stud;
+------------+
| count(rno) |
+------------+
|          6 |
+------------+
1 row in set (0.00 sec)
```

Date Conversion Functions:

```
mysql> create table emp (eno int, doj date);
Query OK, 0 rows affected (0.24 sec)

mysql> insert into emp (eno, doj) values (5001, '2005/12/15');
Query OK, 1 row affected (0.44 sec)

mysql> insert into emp (eno, doj) values (5002, '2006/01/07');
Query OK, 1 row affected (0.22 sec)
```

```
mysql> select * from emp;
+------+------------+
| eno  | doj        |
+------+------------+
| 5001 | 2005-12-15 |
| 5002 | 2006-01-07 |
+------+------------+
2 rows in set (0.02 sec)

mysql> select eno, date_format(doj, '%d/%m/%Y') from emp;
+------+------------------------------+
| eno  | date_format(doj, '%d/%m/%Y') |
+------+------------------------------+
| 5001 | 15/12/2005                   |
| 5002 | 07/01/2006                   |
+------+------------------------------+
2 rows in set (0.08 sec)

mysql> insert into emp values (5003, str_to_date('01/01/2001','%d/%m/%Y'));
Query OK, 1 row affected (0.13 sec)

mysql> insert into emp values (5004, sysdate());
Query OK, 1 row affected, 1 warning (0.31 sec)

Note: sysdate() functions both date and time.

mysql> show warnings;
+-------+------+----------------------------------------+
| Level | Code | Message                                |
+-------+------+----------------------------------------+
| Note  | 1265 | Data truncated for column 'doj' at row 1 |
+-------+------+----------------------------------------+
1 row in set (0.06 sec)

mysql> insert into emp values (5005, date(sysdate()) );
Query OK, 1 row affected (0.47 sec)

mysql> insert into emp values (5006, curdate());
Query OK, 1 row affected (0.05 sec)
```

```
mysql> select * from emp;
+------+------------+
| eno  | doj        |
+------+------------+
| 5001 | 2005-12-15 |
| 5002 | 2006-01-07 |
| 5003 | 2001-01-01 |
| 5004 | 2009-05-02 |
| 5005 | 2009-05-02 |
| 5006 | 2009-05-02 |
+------+------------+
6 rows in set (0.00 sec)

mysql> select curdate();
+------------+
| curdate()  |
+------------+
| 2009-05-02 |
+------------+
1 row in set (0.00 sec)

mysql> select datediff( curdate(), str_to_date('01/04/2009', '%d/%m/%Y') );
+--------------------------------------------------------------+
| datediff( curdate(), str_to_date('01/04/2009', '%d/%m/%Y') ) |
+--------------------------------------------------------------+
|                                                           31 |
+--------------------------------------------------------------+
1 row in set (0.00 sec)

mysql> select datediff( str_to_date('24/04/2009', '%d/%m/%Y'), curdate() );
+--------------------------------------------------------------+
| datediff( str_to_date('24/04/2009', '%d/%m/%Y'), curdate() ) |
+--------------------------------------------------------------+
|                                                           -8 |
+--------------------------------------------------------------+
1 row in set (0.00 sec)
```

Referential Integrity:

```
mysql> create table employee (
    -> id int auto_increment primary key,
    -> empname varchar(20) );
Query OK, 0 rows affected (0.59 sec)
```

```
mysql> create table address (
     -> id int auto_increment primary key,
     -> city   varchar(20),
     -> country varchar(20),
     -> empid int not null,
     -> foreign key (empid) references employee(id) );
Query OK, 0 rows affected (1.03 sec)

mysql> insert into employee (empname) values ('Ibrahim'), ('Kumar');
Query OK, 2 rows affected (0.22 sec)
Records: 2  Duplicates: 0  Warnings: 0

mysql> select * from employee;
+----+---------+
| id | empname |
+----+---------+
|  1 | Ibrahim |
|  2 | Kumar   |
+----+---------+
2 rows in set (0.11 sec)

mysql> insert into address (city, country, empid) values
     -> ('Kuala Lumpur', 'Malaysia', 1),
     -> ('Chennai', 'India', 2);
Query OK, 2 rows affected (0.56 sec)
Records: 2  Duplicates: 0  Warnings: 0
```

Note: It is not allowed to insert a record in child table (address) when its corresponding record not found in parent table (employee). Now, we try to insert empid as 5 (which is not present in employee table).

```
mysql> insert into address (city,country,empid) values
     -> ('Penang', 'Malaysia', 5);
ERROR 1452 (23000): Cannot add or update a child row: a foreign key constraint
     fails (`hdemodb/address`, CONSTRAINT `address_ibfk_1`
FOREIGN KEY (`empid`) REFERENCES `employee` (`id`))
```

Note: It is not allowed to delete a row from parent table while corresponding row present in child table.

```
mysql> delete from employee where id=1;
ERROR 1451 (23000): Cannot delete or update a parent row:
     a foreign key constraint fails (`hdemodb/address`, CONSTRAINT `address_
     ibfk_1`
FOREIGN KEY (`empid`) REFERENCES `employee` (`id`))
```

Note: If the primary key for a record in the parent table changes, all corresponding records in the child table will be modified due to "cascading update" option, and if a record in the parent table is deleted, all corresponding records in the child table will be deleted due to "cascading delete" option.

```
mysql> create table address
     -> (id int auto_increment primary key,
     -> city   varchar(20),
     -> country varchar(20),
     -> empid int not null,
     -> foreign key (empid) references employee(id)
     ->                     on delete cascade
     ->                     on update cascade
     -> ) type=InnoDB;
Query OK, 0 rows affected, 1 warning (0.17 sec)

mysql> select * from employee;
+----+---------+
| id | empname |
+----+---------+
|  1 | Ibrahim |
|  2 | Kumar   |
+----+---------+
2 rows in set (0.19 sec)

mysql> insert into address (city, country, empid) values
     -> ('Kuala Lumpur', 'Malaysia', 1),
     -> ('Chennai', 'India', 2);
Query OK, 2 rows affected (0.06 sec)
Records: 2  Duplicates: 0  Warnings: 0

mysql> select * from address;
+----+--------------+----------+-------+
| id | city         | country  | empid |
+----+--------------+----------+-------+
|  1 | Kuala Lumpur | Malaysia |     1 |
|  2 | Chennai      | India    |     2 |
+----+--------------+----------+-------+
2 rows in set (0.00 sec)

mysql> delete from employee where id=1;
Query OK, 1 row affected (0.05 sec)
```

```
mysql> select * from employee;
+----+---------+
| id | empname |
+----+---------+
|  2 | Kumar   |
+----+---------+
1 row in set (0.00 sec)

mysql> select * from address;
+----+---------+---------+-------+
| id | city    | country | empid |
+----+---------+---------+-------+
|  2 | Chennai | India   |     2 |
+----+---------+---------+-------+
1 row in set (0.00 sec)

mysql> update employee set id=10 where id=2;
Query OK, 1 row affected (0.05 sec)
Rows matched: 1  Changed: 1  Warnings: 0

mysql> select * from employee;
+----+---------+
| id | empname |
+----+---------+
| 10 | Kumar   |
+----+---------+
1 row in set (0.00 sec)

mysql> select * from address;
+----+---------+---------+-------+
| id | city    | country | empid |
+----+---------+---------+-------+
|  2 | Chennai | India   |    10 |
+----+---------+---------+-------+
1 row in set (0.00 sec)
```

Stored Procedures:

`IN` *parameter*

```
mysql> create table st1 (rno int, sname varchar(15));
Query OK, 0 rows affected (0.14 sec)

mysql> insert into st1 values (1000, 'Ibrhaim'),(1001, 'Kannan'),
    (1002,'Navas');
```

```
Query OK, 3 rows affected (0.05 sec)
Records: 3  Duplicates: 0  Warnings: 0

mysql> select * from st1;
+------+---------+
| rno  | sname   |
+------+---------+
| 1000 | Ibrhaim |
| 1001 | Kannan  |
| 1002 | Navas   |
+------+---------+
3 rows in set (0.00 sec)

mysql> drop procedure if exists del;
Query OK, 0 rows affected, 1 warning (0.00 sec)

mysql> delimiter //

mysql> create procedure del(in rollnum int)
    -> begin
    ->   delete from st1 where st1.rno = rollnum;
    -> end
    -> //
Query OK, 0 rows affected (0.00 sec)

mysql> delimiter ;

mysql> call del(1001);
Query OK, 1 row affected (0.06 sec)

mysql> select * from st1;
+------+---------+
| rno  | sname   |
+------+---------+
| 1000 | Ibrhaim |
| 1002 | Navas   |
+------+---------+
2 rows in set (0.00 sec)
```

OUT *parameter*

```
mysql> drop procedure if exists tempconversion;
Query OK, 0 rows affected, 1 warning (0.00 sec)

mysql> delimiter //
```

```
mysql> create procedure tempconversion(in f double, out c double)
    -> begin
    ->  set c = 5.0 / 9.0 * (f - 32.0);
    -> end;
    -> //
Query OK, 0 rows affected (0.00 sec)

mysql> select @tempf;
+--------+
| @tempf |
+--------+
| 98.4   |
+--------+
1 row in set (0.00 sec)

mysql> select @tempc;
+--------+
| @tempc |
+--------+
| 0      |
+--------+
1 row in set (0.00 sec)

mysql> call tempconversion(@tempf, @tempc);
Query OK, 0 rows affected (0.00 sec)

mysql> select @tempf;
+--------+
| @tempf |
+--------+
| 98.4   |
+--------+
1 row in set (0.00 sec)

mysql> select @tempc;
+-----------------+
| @tempc          |
+-----------------+
| 36.888888888889 |
+-----------------+
1 row in set (0.03 sec)
```

INOUT parameter:

```
mysql> drop procedure if exists netpay;
Query OK, 0 rows affected, 1 warning (0.00 sec)

mysql> delimiter //

mysql> create procedure netpay (inout salary double)
    -> begin
    ->   declare deductions double;
    ->   set deductions = salary * 0.15;
    ->   set salary = salary - deductions;
    -> end;
    -> //
Query OK, 0 rows affected (0.00 sec)

mysql> delimiter ;

mysql> set @pay = 78000.0;
Query OK, 0 rows affected (0.00 sec)

mysql> select @pay;
+---------+
| @pay    |
+---------+
| 78000.0 |
+---------+
1 row in set (0.00 sec)

mysql> call netpay(@pay);
Query OK, 0 rows affected (0.00 sec)

mysql> select @pay;
+-------+
| @pay  |
+-------+
| 66300 |
+-------+
1 row in set (0.00 sec)
```

Stored Function:

```
mysql> drop function if exists factorial;
Query OK, 0 rows affected, 1 warning (0.00 sec)

mysql> delimiter //
```

```
mysql> create function factorial(n int) returns int
     -> begin
     ->  declare f int default 1;
     ->  while n > 0 do
     ->   set f = f * n;
     ->   set n = n - 1;
     ->  end while;
     ->  return f;
     -> end;
     -> //
Query OK, 0 rows affected (0.00 sec)

mysql> delimiter ;

mysql> select factorial(4);
+--------------+
| factorial(4) |
+--------------+
|           24 |
+--------------+
1 row in set (0.00 sec)
```

Cursor manipulation:

The following PL/SQL calculates and updates required student data.

```
mysql> create table student
     -> ( rollnum    int,
     ->   name       varchar(15),
     ->   mark1      int,
     ->   mark2      int,
     ->   mark3      int,
     ->   total      int,
     ->   average    double,
     ->   result     varchar(4),
     ->   class      varchar(15)  );
Query OK, 0 rows affected (0.13 sec)

mysql> desc student;
+---------+-------------+------+-----+---------+-------+
| Field   | Type        | Null | Key | Default | Extra |
+---------+-------------+------+-----+---------+-------+
| rollnum | int(11)     | YES  |     | NULL    |       |
| name    | varchar(15) | YES  |     | NULL    |       |
| mark1   | int(11)     | YES  |     | NULL    |       |
```

```
| mark2    | int(11)     | YES  |     | NULL    |       |
| mark3    | int(11)     | YES  |     | NULL    |       |
| total    | int(11)     | YES  |     | NULL    |       |
| average  | double      | YES  |     | NULL    |       |
| result   | varchar(4)  | YES  |     | NULL    |       |
| class    | varchar(15) | YES  |     | NULL    |       |
+----------+-------------+------+-----+---------+-------+
9 rows in set (0.03 sec)

mysql> insert into student (rollnum, name, mark1, mark2, mark3) values
    -> (1001, 'Ibrahim', 90, 93, 98),
    -> (1002, 'Kumar', 60, 65, 64),
    -> (1003, 'Ajay', 49, 80, 78),
    -> (1004, 'Nitin', 52, 55, 54);
Query OK, 4 rows affected (0.06 sec)
Records: 4  Duplicates: 0  Warnings: 0

mysql> select * from student;
+---------+---------+-------+-------+-------+-------+---------+--------+-------+
| rollnum | name    | mark1 | mark2 | mark3 | total | average | result | class |
+---------+---------+-------+-------+-------+-------+---------+--------+-------+
|    1001 | Ibrahim |    90 |    93 |    98 |  NULL |    NULL | NULL   | NULL  |
|    1002 | Kumar   |    60 |    65 |    64 |  NULL |    NULL | NULL   | NULL  |
|    1003 | Ajay    |    49 |    80 |    78 |  NULL |    NULL | NULL   | NULL  |
|    1004 | Nitin   |    52 |    55 |    54 |  NULL |    NULL | NULL   | NULL  |
+---------+---------+-------+-------+-------+-------+---------+--------+-------+
4 rows in set (0.00 sec)
```

Store the following content in the file marklist.sql (under C: drive).

```
drop procedure if exists marklist;

delimiter //

create procedure marklist()
begin
    declare rnum, m1, m2, m3, mltotal  int;
    declare mlaverage                  numeric(5, 2);
    declare mlresult                   varchar(4);
    declare mlclass                    varchar(15);
    declare recordNotFound          boolean default false;

    declare c cursor for select rollnum, mark1, mark2, mark3 from student;
    declare continue handler for not found set recordNotFound=true;
```

```
    open c;
    L1: loop
      fetch c into rnum, m1, m2, m3;
      if recordNotFound then
        leave L1;
      end if;

      set mltotal = m1 + m2 + m3;
      set mlaverage = mltotal / 3;

      if (m1 >= 50 and m2 >= 50 and m3 >= 50) then
        set mlresult = 'PASS';
      else
        set mlresult = 'FAIL';
      end if;

      if mlresult = 'PASS' then
        case
          when mlaverage >= 85 then set mlclass = 'DISTINCTION';
          when mlaverage >= 60 then set mlclass = 'FIRST';
          else set mlclass = 'SECOND';
        end case;
      else
        set mlclass = ' --- ';
      end if;

      update student set total = mltotal, average = mlaverage,
                   result = mlresult, class = mlclass
                   where rollnum = rnum;
    end loop L1;
    close c;
    commit;
end //

delimiter ;
```

Executing the above procedure:

```
mysql> source C:\marklist.sql
Query OK, 0 rows affected (0.00 sec)

Query OK, 0 rows affected (0.00 sec)
```

```
mysql> call marklist();
Query OK, 0 rows affected, 2 warnings (0.00 sec)

mysql> select * from student;
+---------+---------+-------+-------+-------+-------+---------+--------+-------------+
| rollnum | name    | mark1 | mark2 | mark3 | total | average | result | class       |
+---------+---------+-------+-------+-------+-------+---------+--------+-------------+
|    1001 | Ibrahim |    90 |    93 |    98 |   281 |   93.67 | PASS   | DISTINCTION |
|    1002 | Kumar   |    60 |    65 |    64 |   189 |      63 | PASS   | FIRST       |
|    1003 | Ajay    |    49 |    80 |    78 |   207 |      69 | FAIL   |  ---        |
|    1004 | Nitin   |    52 |    55 |    54 |   161 |   53.67 | PASS   | SECOND      |
+---------+---------+-------+-------+-------+-------+---------+--------+-------------+
4 rows in set (0.00 sec)
```

Trigger:

```
mysql> create table marklist
     -> ( rollnum int primary key,
     ->   mark1   int,
     ->   mark2   int,
     ->   mark3   int
     -> );
Query OK, 0 rows affected (0.16 sec)

mysql> create table passcount (count int default 0);
Query OK, 0 rows affected (0.09 sec)

mysql> create trigger pass_count_trigger
     ->  before insert on marklist
     ->  for each row
     -> begin
     ->  if new.mark1 >= 50 and new.mark2 >= 50 and new.mark3 >= 50 then
     ->   update passcount set count = count + 1;
     ->  end if;
     -> end;
     -> //
Query OK, 0 rows affected (0.00 sec)

mysql> insert into passcount (count) values (0);
Query OK, 1 row affected (0.03 sec)

mysql> select * from passcount;
```

```
+-------+
| count |
+-------+
|     0 |
+-------+
1 row in set (0.00 sec)

mysql> insert into marklist (rollnum, mark1, mark2, mark3) values
    -> (1001, 50, 60, 70),
    -> (1002, 40, 50, 60),
    -> (1003, 70, 80, 90),
    -> (1004, 10, 20, 30);
Query OK, 4 rows affected (0.06 sec)
Records: 4  Duplicates: 0  Warnings: 0

mysql> select * from marklist;
+---------+-------+-------+-------+
| rollnum | mark1 | mark2 | mark3 |
+---------+-------+-------+-------+
|    1001 |    50 |    60 |    70 |
|    1002 |    40 |    50 |    60 |
|    1003 |    70 |    80 |    90 |
|    1004 |    10 |    20 |    30 |
+---------+-------+-------+-------+
4 rows in set (0.00 sec)

mysql> select * from passcount;
+-------+
| count |
+-------+
|     2 |
+-------+
1 row in set (0.00 sec)
```

SUMMARY

This chapter started with the MySQL installation procedure. Important data-definition, data-manipulation, transaction-control, and MySQL programs are explained with illustrations. A set of frequently used built-in functions are given by their operations wise. The latest features of MySQL, stored procedures/functions, triggers, are explained with example code. The readers are further advised to use SQL client software to interact with MySQL in GUI mode, which makes easy to work.

INDEX

U

V

W